Cambridge Elements ≡

Elements in Organization Theory
edited by
Nelson Phillips
UC Santa Barbara
Royston Greenwood
Imperial College London, University of Alberta

FAMILY FIRM

A Distinctive Form of Organization

Evelyn Micelotta
University of Ottawa

Carlotta Benedetti
Politecnico di Milano School of Management, Milano, Italy

Paola Rovelli
Free University of Bozen-Bolzano, Bolzano, Italy

CAMBRIDGE
UNIVERSITY PRESS

Shaftesbury Road, Cambridge CB2 8EA, United Kingdom

One Liberty Plaza, 20th Floor, New York, NY 10006, USA

477 Williamstown Road, Port Melbourne, VIC 3207, Australia

314–321, 3rd Floor, Plot 3, Splendor Forum, Jasola District Centre,
New Delhi – 110025, India

103 Penang Road, #05–06/07, Visioncrest Commercial, Singapore 238467

Cambridge University Press is part of Cambridge University Press & Assessment,
a department of the University of Cambridge.

We share the University's mission to contribute to society through the pursuit of
education, learning and research at the highest international levels of excellence.

www.cambridge.org
Information on this title: www.cambridge.org/9781009087612

DOI: 10.1017/9781009083461

First published 2023

A catalogue record for this publication is available from the British Library.

ISBN 978-1-009-08761-2 Paperback
ISSN 2397-947X (online)
ISSN 2514-3859 (print)

Family Firm

A Distinctive Form of Organization

Elements in Organization Theory

DOI: 10.1017/9781009083461
First published online: January 2023

Evelyn Micelotta
University of Ottawa

Carlotta Benedetti
Politecnico di Milano School of Management, Milano, Italy

Paola Rovelli
Free University of Bozen-Bolzano, Bolzano, Italy

Author for correspondence: Evelyn Micelotta, Micelotta@telfer.uottawa.ca

Abstract: Family firms are organizations where the influence of the family over the firm and distinctive configurations of ownership, management, and governance create unique opportunities and challenges. Organization theory (OT) offers a wide array of theoretical concepts to understand the inner working of family firms and their role in society. Family business (FB) research has also pointed at singularities of these organizations, which offer insights for extending organization theories. Yet, cross-fertilization between FB research and OT studies remains limited. In this Element, the authors reinvigorate calls to explore avenues to further integrate these two research fields. They present the FB literature in management journals and categorize these papers based on four types of theoretical contribution: Embedded, Integrative, Challenger, and Generalized. The authors discuss opportunities for dialogue between FB and OT for each type in three research domains: (i) managing hybridity; (ii) mastering tensions, dualities, and paradoxes; and (iii) modeling time and temporality.

This Element also has a video abstract: www.cambridge.org/Organization Theory _ Evelyn Micelotta_abstract

Keywords: organization theory, family business, hybridity, paradoxes, temporality

ISBNs: 9781009087612 (PB), 9781009083461 (OC)
ISSNs: 2397-947X (online), 2514-3859 (print)

Contents

A tenet of organizational theory is that one can explain the prevalence and distribution of an organizational form with respect to the fit of that form to its environment. By these standards, the family enterprise must be a remarkably efficient and robust organizational form: it is the world's most common form of economic organization and, as noted by La Porta et al. (1999), family-controlled corporations dominate the global economic landscape.

Rafael La Porta, Florencio Lopez-De-Silanes, and Andrei Shleifer,
"Corporate Ownership around the World"

1 Family Business Research and Organization Studies

1.1 The Objective and Organization of the Element

Family firms are a dominant form of organization across the globe, in emerging as well as in established economies, and play a prominent role in the global economic landscape (Zellweger, 2017). These organizations are also ubiquitous. Recent estimates indicate that 65–90 percent of all companies in the world are family owned, including more than one-third of the S&P 500 companies (Claessens et al., 2000; Faccio & Lang, 2002; La Porta et al., 1999; Zellweger et al., 2015). With their emphasis and commitment to long-term ownership, family values and identity, sustainability, and a desire for the firm to endure across generations, family businesses are a distinctive organizational form compared to nonfamily firms (Gomez-Mejia et al., 2011). Indeed, the intersection of family ownership and business presents unique challenges to these companies that seek to balance economic and noneconomic goals and to preserve the socioemotional wealth (SEW) of both the family and the business (Gomez-Mejia et al., 2007). Examining the organizational features and strategic postures of these organizations is therefore essential to understand the organizations that surround us and their critical role in society.

As these organizational forms are so ubiquitous and impactful, family businesses should be consistently on the radar of organizational scholars. And yet, they are not. Organization theory and family business (FB) research have seemingly developed on parallel paths, with only occasional and sporadic crossovers. Organization theory has a long-standing tradition that traces back to the early sociological efforts to understand the large new organizations that proliferated in the late nineteenth and early twentieth centuries (Hinings & Meyer, 2018). The interest in the rationalization of society focused scholarly attention on the rational–legal authority system and the bureaucratic form (Weber, 1947). Other prevalent forms of organizing, such as the traditional authority system (that underpins family firms) or the charismatic form based on strong leadership, were pushed to the background, even though some of the largest and most influential companies at the time were indeed family firms (e.g., DuPont and

Ford). As Hinings and Meyer (2018, p. 17) note, "there has been little analysis of . . . traditional authority systems in organization theory generally, although there is considerable study of family business as a relatively specialized area (cf. Family Business Review)." As a result, theories of organizations and managerial insights have been mostly derived from the examination of nonfamily corporations. The impact of different types of ownership and control structures has not been systematically factored in.

This trajectory has not significantly changed in the modern days of OT. Organizational scholars tend to consider family firms as an interesting empirical setting on which to build theoretical insights. This is very reasonable. As shown by research in health care and professional service organizations (see other titles in the Elements in Organization Theory series), organizational theories can be fruitfully applied to organizations with distinctive features. This approach is generative but assumes that OT is positioned on a higher level in the discipline hierarchy. Whether OT is foundational to our understanding of FB remains an open question, worthy of dialogue. In this Element, we are interested in exploring reciprocal relationships, where the analysis of unique forms of organizing generates new theories of organizations or at least highlights important boundary conditions. A good example is research on social enterprises, which spurred new theories of hybrid organizing. We suggest that the peculiarities of family ownership and management make them excellent empirical settings *and* open the possibility for new, or at least revised, theories of organizations.

Somewhat independently from OT, the family business research field has seen a rapid growth in the past decades, but its theoretical maturity is far from being reached (Holt et al., 2018; Neubaum & Micelotta, 2021; Payne, 2018). The field started with a distinctive "practitioner" flavor and has only relatively recently acquired the legitimacy of an academic area of research (Sharma et al., 2012; Stewart & Miner, 2011). For the past twenty-five years, researchers have dedicated efforts to develop theoretical insights about family businesses. Scholars, however, still debate about whether the field of family business is anything other than a unique – although quite prevalent – context of study. This is due to the lack of clear boundaries and comprehensive conceptual frameworks to define the field (Payne, 2018), as well as the need for original theories related to the context of family enterprises (Reay & Whetten, 2011).

Although advancing the theoretical development of the field is necessary, the task is challenging. Grasping the peculiar dynamics that characterize family enterprises can be problematic as they are generated at the intersection of two intertwined but idiosyncratic systems: the family and the business. Indeed, the field has been referred to as one of paradoxes and tensions (e.g., Zahra & Sharma, 2004), which denotes a "wide variety of contradictory yet interwoven elements: perspectives, feelings, messages, demands, identities, interests, or practices" (Lewis, 2000, p. 761). Family business research is therefore an intrinsically multidisciplinary field, where scholars rely on various theoretical frameworks to address relevant phenomena and research questions. The field comprises a large set of interrelated subfields linked together by the common thread of the family's involvement in the ownership, governance, and management of their businesses (Yu et al., 2012).

Thus far, family business researchers have drawn primarily on theories from economics and strategy (e.g., agency theory, behavioral theory of the firm) and conducted mostly quantitative studies. Only recently, the field has begun to draw upon a wider array of theories of organizations, including from sociology and culture (Sasaki et al., 2019), as well as adopting a wider array of qualitative approaches (Fletcher et al., 2016; Micelotta et al., 2020). Such variety has importantly enhanced our understanding of these organizations and their complex interrelationships across levels of analysis (Chirico & Salvato, 2016). However, integration of family business research and organization studies is still occasional. Many opportunities to create a strong and consistent research program around this integration remain untapped (Salvato et al., 2019). Interestingly, the family business field has created bridges with the field of entrepreneurship, as indicated by the growing number of publications, journal special issues, and conference themes dedicated to family business research in entrepreneurship outlets. The field of entrepreneurship has experienced a similar trajectory of development and these commonalities may have enhanced the opportunities for dialogue. Conversely, the cross-fertilization of family business with organization studies dwarfs in comparison (Aldrich & Cliff, 2003; Salvato et al., 2019).

In this Element, we have two goals. First, we introduce the FB and OT audiences to one another because they may have little or no familiarity with their respective areas of research. The interest for cross-domain research is growing, as are research and publication opportunities. Yet, there is still a divide between the two fields, which will grow if the next generations of researchers become more specialized. Doctoral students in OT are well versed in organization theories, but they may not know how much research has been done in the family business domain. Similarly, students in the family business field may lack deep exposure to organization theories in their doctoral courses. The interdisciplinary nature and theoretical openness of FB research make the field exciting, but it is likely harder to navigate for students who need to master a wide array of theories to address their (family business) research questions.

This is also a good time to renew calls made in the past by a number of family business (e.g., Sharma, 2004) and organization studies researchers (Hjorth & Dawson, 2016). FB research has matured from a specialized research area where practitioners' knowledge was central to a legitimate field with theory development at its core. Research focused on family business firms has grown substantially in the past few years, not only in size (i.e., number of published papers) but also in quality (Rovelli et al., 2021; Sharma, 2004; Xi et al., 2015). Specialist journals (e.g., *Family Business Review*) are becoming increasingly demanding in terms of theoretical contribution, whereas generalist management journals are increasingly interested in theory and insights about family businesses. Opportunities for theoretical generalization are more evident and the convergence of standards provides a growing number of outlets where bridging conversations can occur.

Our second goal is to encourage the integration between FB and OT by suggesting promising areas of overlap that can highlight and reinforce the usefulness of an OT lens. There is a growing appetite in the FB domain for management lenses that can help scholars and practitioners better understand and support strategies and behaviors of family businesses. The recent trend, however, has been to look at insights from outside the OT field. For instance, there is a keen interest in family science (Jaskiewicz et al., 2017b), history (Suddaby & Jaskiewicz, 2020), or organizational behavior (OB) and social psychology (De Massis & Foss, 2018) to shed light on the foundations of family business behaviors and the intricate dynamics between family and business. Although these theoretical linkages are extremely useful, they represent a warning that OT may become increasingly disconnected from the FB field and perhaps been perceived as less relevant and useful. Not dissimilar from other boundary-spanning streams of research highlighted in the Elements series (e.g., Muzio et al., 2019; Reay et al., 2021), we strongly believe that the intersection of FB and OT is full of theoretical possibilities. We seek to jumpstart this conversation (again) and hopefully stimulate researchers to continue to explore and experiment with research that spans boundaries and reaches across the FB–OT theoretical aisle.

This Element is organized as follows. In Section 2, we introduce the field of family business and describe its evolution through an overview of the family business literature (908 relevant papers) published in the time frame 1995–2020. We highlight the topics that have intrigued family business scholars as well as the theoretical lenses they have drawn upon with a longitudinal perspective. In Section 3, we begin to explore the intersection of organizational studies and family business research by analyzing a subsample of seventy-seven family business papers published in high-quality management journals listed in the FT50 and classified as ABS 4/4*. We examine their theoretical contributions based on two dimensions – contextual orientation and target audience. At the intersection of these two dimensions, we find four types of papers: embedded, integrative, challenger, and generalized. In Section 4, we identify research opportunities between organization studies and family business research. We summarize the literature and offer research questions to stimulate cross-fertilization in three research foci: (i) managing hybridity; (ii) mastering tensions, dualities, and paradoxes; and (iii) modeling time and temporality. Finally, in Section 5, we offer our concluding thoughts.

1.2 Methodological Note

A methodological note is useful to explain the scope of our review. Our analyzes are based on a literature search of relevant family business articles conducted by the authors in September 2021. We followed a systematic approach to retrieve relevant papers. First, we defined a set of keywords that capture the family business field of research (i.e., *family business**, *family firm**, *family enter**, *family entre**, *business famil**, *family influence, family control**, *family own**, *family manag**). Using these keywords, we focused on research published – or in press – in academic journals. We selected two journals dedicated to family business research – that is, *Family Business Review* and *Journal of Family Business Strategy* – and the (twenty-five) journals ranking 4/4* in the fields of entrepreneurship and small business management; general management, ethics, gender, and social responsibility; international business and area studies; innovation, management development, and education; organizational studies, social sciences, and strategy of the *Academic Journal Guide (AJG) 2018* ranking of the Chartered Association of Business Schools (CABS). This ranking is widely used by business schools to assess the rigor and quality of journals. Third, we restricted our search to articles written in English published since 1995. The founding year of *Family Business Review* – the first outlet dedicated to family business research – is 1988. We chose 1995 because articles started to be published in an academic format (rather than essays) in that year.

We searched our keywords in the title, abstract, or keywords of papers published in the selected journals using Scopus, the largest database of peer-reviewed literature. The search resulted in 1,523 articles. Two authors independently evaluated the relevance of each article by reading their title and abstract, and, when necessary, the full paper. Unclear cases and disagreements were discussed among the authors. This procedure led to a final sample of 908 articles on family business-related issues.

2 A Brief History of Research in the Family Business Domain

2.1 The Academic Field of Family Business Research

Family businesses are recognized today as major players in the global economy. In a constantly evolving and vibrant environment, firms run by families have managed to survive and thrive by using their distinctive features to their own advantage. Their hybrid nature, built on the two subsystems of family and business, makes these firms working organisms characterized by long-term sustainability (Zellweger et al., 2012a) – ability to preserve value across generations (Nordqvist & Zellweger, 2010), a strong socioemotional attachment (Gomez-Mejia et al., 2007, 2011), and a history that comes together with values, culture, and tradition (Suddaby & Jaskiewicz, 2020). Today, scholars recognize both the ubiquity of family firms and their complexity (Sharma et al., 2012). However, this has not always been the case. Publications on family firms started to appear in management journals only in 1990. Since 1995, the number of papers published per year has rapidly increased (more than 2,000 articles published in the 1990s and more than 4,000 articles published between 2010 and 2014). Academic interest in this peculiar type of organization has also grown, as shown by the increase in management top-tier journals that now welcome studies in this field (Sharma et al., 2012; Stewart & Miner, 2011). Compared with OT, however, family business is still a relatively young research domain. Some of its foundational constructs (e.g., SEW) are still under scrutiny, and efforts to further specify the boundaries and direction of research in the field are needed.

2.2 What Are Family Firms?

The definition of family business continues to be a crucial point of discussion within the family business community. New definitions of family business are proposed, and definitional ambiguities persist, even after all the years researchers have spent systematically investigating family firm characteristics, goals, and behaviors (Chua et al., 1999; Litz, 2008; Upton et al., 1993). Initially, researchers adopted an operational definition of family business using family involvement in a firm's ownership and management as the main criteria for differentiating family firms from nonfamily organizations. However, researchers struggled to separate family from nonfamily firms as family involvement and family ownership were often differently interpreted and perceived by the firms themselves (Chua et al., 1999; Villalonga & Amit, 2006; Westhead & Cowling, 1998). Accordingly, researchers have increasingly recognized the need to distinguish between definitions that are theoretically based and those that are more operational in nature (Chua et al., 1999).

The approaches used to define family firms have been divided into *involvement* and *essence* approaches (Chrisman et al., 2005). The involvement approach adopts ownership, governance or directorship, management, and the involvement of multiple family generations as the most common defining criteria. The essence approach proposes that theoretical definitions of family firms should be based on the essence of family influence, including intention for intra-family succession, self-identification as a family firm, unique and synergistic resources, and the preservation of socioemotional values among the defining criteria (Chrisman et al., 2012; Hoy & Sharma, 2006). The involvement and essence approaches are firm-centered approaches to define the family business. That is, the existence of the business is assumed, and the definition concerns the family's role and influence in the business. A family-centered approach has emerged, which considers equally the family and the business side of the family–business dyad, including the involvement and management in the household (Heck & Stafford, 2001; Winter et al., 1998). Although progress has been made, defining the family remains a challenging task that would greatly benefit from further refinement.

Finally, a recent stream of research has shifted the focus from considering family firms as a homogeneous group to a heterogeneous one. Not all family firms share the same attributes and characteristics (Chua et al., 2012; Sharma & Nordqvist, 2008; Villalonga & Amit, 2006). Hence, it becomes important to redefine family firms based on all the relevant dimensions along which they may vary from each other, in addition to their nonfamily counterparts. Among these dimensions, family firms widely vary in the way they deal with temporality. Differently from other types of organizations, family firms are indeed not just influenced by time, but they express their agency through temporal work by interpreting past traditions in the present to guide the future behaviors (Suddaby & Jaskiewicz, 2020). Family business tensions are indeed often intergenerational in nature and, thus, rest on the family business's capacity to integrate past, present, and future within the broader tension of continuity versus change.

We summarize approaches and definitions in the family business literature in Table 1.

2.3 Evolution of Family Business Research

Our literature search found 908 articles on family business-related issues published in top-tier journals over the years 1995–2020; these papers are associated with 71,524 citations (corresponding to 78.77 citations per paper) at the time this analysis was conducted. The number of papers published per year has rapidly increased over time (Figure 1, blue line). This reflects the increased interest in family firms as a peculiar type of organization, not only by individual scholars but also by a wider group of management journals (Table 2).

The analysis of the trend of publications per year revealed three temporal brackets that, following Jaskiewicz et al. (2020), we labeled: emergence

Table 1 Definitions of family firms proposed in the literature

Definition of family firm	Reference
The owner/CEO identifies the firm as family firm	De Massis et al. (2021); Harveston et al. (1997); Mahto et al. (2013)
The CEO is a member of the family and there is more than one generation actively involved in the firm	Calabrò et al. (2013)
The founder or a family member is an officer, a director, or the owner of at least 20 percent of the firm (individually or as a group), and the CEO identifies the firm as a family firm and affirms that the ownership will most likely pass to heirs	Caselli and Di Giuli (2010)
At least two family members are employed in the firm and the ownership is in the hands of the family	Eddleston et al. (2008); Kellermanns and Eddleston (2006)
A family owns at least 5 percent of the voting stocks of the firm	Berrone et al. (2010)
A family owns at least 20 percent of the firm and a family member is involved in the board of directors	Tiscini and Raoli (2013)
A family owns more than 25 percent of the firm	De Massis et al. (2013)
A family owns at least 25 percent of the firm and the CEO is a member of the family	Ansari et al. (2014)
A family owns at least 25 percent of the firm and at least two members of the family participate in the management of the firm and/or the board of directors	García-Ramos and García-Olalla (2011)
A family owns at least 50 percent of the firm	Cruz and Nordqvist (2012); Ling and Kellermanns (2010); Sciascia et al. (2012)
A family owns at least 50 percent of the firm. The threshold is reduced to 25 percent for listed firms	Miller et al. (2013); Naldi et al. (2013)

Table 1 (cont.)

Definition of family firm	Reference
A family owns at least 50 percent of the firm. The threshold is reduced to 30 percent for listed firms	De Massis et al. (2021); Minichilli et al. (2010)
A family owns at least 51 percent of the firm and there are family members on the board of directors or in management	Basco (2013)

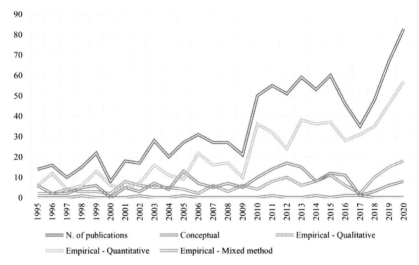

Figure 1 Publication trends in the literature on family business.
Source: The Authors

(1995–2009), adolescence (2010–14), and adulthood (2015–20). The first bracket illustrates the emergence of the field (see also Rovelli et al., 2021). In this phase, family business research established itself in the management field. Scholarly production consisted in 20.07 papers per year, and this average remained stable throughout the fifteen years of this period. In aggregate, the papers that received the highest number of citations are those published between 2000 and 2009, with an average of 146.15 citations per paper compared to 81.91 citations per paper in the previous five years. Two of the top-three most cited works in this phase have been published after 2000: Gomez-Mejia et al. (2007) in *Administrative Science Quarterly*, with 1,571 citations, and Schulze et al. (2001) in *Organization Science*, with 1,252 citations; these are followed by Habbershon and Williams (1999) in *Family*

Table 2 Journals that published research on family business and related publication trends

Journal	No. of pubs	Emergence			Adolescence	Adulthood
		1995–99	2000–04	2005–09	2010–14	2015–20
Academy of Management Journal	10	-	3	-	4	3
Academy of Management Review	3	-	1	-	1	1
Administrative Science Quarterly	5	-	1	1	1	2
American Sociological Review	2	1	-	1	-	-
British Journal of Management	12	-	1	1	4	6
Business Ethics Quarterly	4	-	-	-	4	-
Entrepreneurship: Theory and Practice	131	-	4	24	53	50
Family Business Review	378	73	61	85	97	62
Human Relations	5	-	-	1	2	2
Journal of Business Venturing	33	2	13	4	10	4
Journal of Family Business Strategy	200	-	-	-	106	94
Journal of International Business Studies	13	-	-	4	3	6
Journal of Management	8	-	-	-	2	6
Journal of Management Studies	28	-	2	6	13	7
Journal of Product Innovation Management	13	-	-	-	5	8
Journal of World Business	13	-	1	2	3	7

Leadership Quarterly	2	-	-	1	1	-
Organization Science	8	-	1	2	4	1
Organization Studies	13	1	3	1	1	7
Research Policy	4	-	-	2	2	
Strategic Entrepreneurship Journal	7	-	-	4	3	
Strategic Management Journal	16	-	-	8	8	
	908	77	91	133	328	279

Business Review, with 992 citations. Gomez-Mejia et al.'s paper (2007) is the famous "Spanish olive mills paper" that introduced the notion of SEW to management scholars. The key idea presented in the paper is that family ownership matters, as the primary reference point for these organizations is the loss of their SEW. Contrary to the predictions of the behavioral theory of the firm at the time, the study claims that family firms are willing to accept significant risks to avoid losses to SEW. The concept of SEW is one of the key tenets of research in family firms and a fertile ground for debates and refinements. The paper by Schulze et al. (2001) represented another significant step in family business research. The authors introduced "altruism" in agency theory as a key element in family businesses that had not been considered in prior economic models. They show how altruism exacerbates agency problems experienced by privately held, owner-managed firms. Finally, the paper by Habbershon and Williams (1999) exposed family business scholars to another big theory – the resource-based view (RBV) of the firm – and opened the door to a strategic view of a cornerstone of research in the family business domain: familiness. Overall, these three contributions have been pivotal in providing family business research with a scaffolding of theoretical concepts that are still very important today.

The main outlet for family business research in the emergence phase has been the journal *Family Business Review*. Founded in 1988, *Family Business Review* is the first journal dedicated to family business research. During the emergence phase, when this line of research was beginning to establish itself, this journal allowed family business scholars to have a suitable place to share their insights. *Family Business Review* has published 219 articles between 1995 and 2009. Other journals have published family business research in this time frame, but in a very limited number, with an average of 5.86 papers. Since 2000 two other journals have stepped into the field: *Journal of Business Venturing*, with nineteen papers published on this topic between 1995 and 2009, and *Entrepreneurship: Theory and Practice*, with four papers in 2000–04 and an impressive growth to twenty-four in 2005–09. The second journal dedicated to family business – *Journal of Family Business Strategy* – was founded in 2010, year that marks the beginning of a new phase of research in this field.

The years following the emergence phase can be divided in two brackets, namely, adolescence – between 2010 and 2015 – and adulthood – between 2016 and 2020. As clearly visible in Figure 1, the transition to the adolescence phase is marked by a significant increase in the average number of papers published per year, from 20.07 to 54.67. In the six-year adolescence phase, a total of 328 papers were published on family firms related issues (36.12 percent of the total sample), with a total of 23,733 citations and 72.36 citations per paper, so far; these are relatively high numbers compared to the previous phase, which suggests that this stream of research has become more legitimate and rallied a large community of scholars. The top-three cited papers in this phase are those by Berrone et al. (2012) in *Family Business Review*, with 838 citations, Berrone et al. (2010) in *Administrative Science Quarterly*, with 700 citations, and Chrisman and Patel (2012) in *Academy of Management Journal*, with 566 citations. The paper by Berrone et al. (2012) is a theoretical essay that "makes the case for the socio-emotional wealth (SEW) approach as the potential dominant paradigm in the family business field." The authors consolidated their collective insights about this framework for the family business community, tackling definitional and operationalization issues. The second paper, also by Berrone et al., represents another example of the theoretical development of the SEW construct. In this empirical paper, the authors speak to the issue of how firms respond to institutional pressures (precisely corporate social responsibility (CSR)) and offer support to the proposition that family firms behave differently from nonfamily firms, because of their desire to protect their SEW. Finally, the paper by Chrisman and Patel (2012) represents another example of family business scholars conversing with a broader audience. The paper challenges the incompatible predictions offered by the behavioral theory of the firm about R&D investments. They show that ownership matters by adding insights from the myopic loss aversion framework, which is better suitable to predict the behaviors of these companies. Overall, the publication of these papers in top management journals has significantly contributed to bringing family business research into mainstream journals and paved the way for additional publications and more opportunities for research.

The adolescence phase is marked by the founding of the *Journal of Family Business Strategy*, which published 106 papers (Table 2), followed by *Family Business Review*, with ninety-seven publications. Following the increasing trend of the emergence phase, family business publications in *Entrepreneurship: Theory and Practice* kept growing, with fifty-three articles published. This trend confirms the growing overlap between the interests of the family business community and the entrepreneurship community, which has helped this journal to establish itself as a prestigious outlet for family business research. Other two journals worth mentioning are the *Journal of Management Studies*, with thirteen papers published, and the *Journal of Business Venturing*, with ten articles. The remaining outlets published an average of 3.06 papers per year.

The third and last phase covers the years 2016–20. As depicted by the blue line in Figure 1, family business research suffered a slight decline in the number of publications in 2016 (forty-six papers) and 2017 (thirty-five papers), to see further growth from 2018, to 83 papers published in 2020. We called this phase adulthood. So far, 279 articles have been published in this phase, covering the 30.73 percent of the entire sample analyzed. To date, the top-three cited papers in this phase are Debicki et al. (2016) in *Journal of Family Business Strategy* (235 citations), De Massis et al. (2018) in *Journal of Product Innovation Management* (255 citations), and Gomez-Mejia et al. (2018) in *Journal of Management* (254 citations). The topics of these papers show a persistent interest in the concept of SEW, but also the exploration of a wide range of scholarly interests, such as innovation and merger and acquisitions. The paper by Debicki et al. (2016) offers the development of the SEW importance scale (SEWi), thus showing that SEW remains a primary theoretical lens to explain family firms' behaviors, and strategies and issues of measurements are at the forefront of scholarly interest. Gomez-Mejia et al. (2018) rely on this perspective to understand what drives acquisition strategies of family firms with a mixed-gamble approach. Finally, the paper by De Massis et al. (2018) looks at innovation in family firms. Through a study of highly successful German firms in innovative domains, the paper reveals the traits that allow them to overcome resource scarcity, to efficiently orchestrate their resources to innovate and outcompete their industry peers.

Interestingly, compared to the previous two phases, fewer articles have been published in *Family Business Review*. The *Journal of Family Business Strategy* and *Entrepreneurship: Theory and Practice* remained stable with ninety-four and fifty papers, respectively. Other journals published an average of 4.56 articles per year. Observing in more detail the journals' publication trends in Table 2, besides *Family Business Review, Journal of Family Business Strategy, Entrepreneurship: Theory and Practice*, six other journals displayed family business research, with at least five papers published on average in the adolescence and adulthood phase and at least ten papers published since 2010: *Journal of Management Studies, Strategic Management Journal, Journal of Business Venturing, Journal of Product Innovation Management, British Journal of Management*, and *Journal of World Business*.

Going back to the trend shown in Figure 1, it is useful to point out the nature of the research conducted by family business scholars. The field is dominated by empirical, rather than conceptual, research, with 726 empirical papers published, corresponding to 79.96 percent of the sample. The 62.67 percent of these works (455 papers) focused only on family firms, while the remaining 37.60 percent (273 papers) compared family firm with their nonfamily counterparts. Most of this empirical research adopted quantitative methodologies (yellow line in Figure 1, 560 papers), whereas a lower number of papers in our sample adopts qualitative methodologies (grey line, 159 papers). Both subsamples of papers follow the same trend of the overall sample. Only seven studies have adopted a mixed methodology. Finally, relatively less effort has been dedicated to conceptual works (orange line, 182 papers, 20.04 percent of the sample).

2.4 Research Trends in Family Business Research

After looking at the evolution of the field in terms of research production and outlets, we examine how family business research has evolved in terms of topics and themes investigated. We build on the paper by Rovelli et al. (2021), who recently analyzed the first thirty years of scholarly production in *Family Business Review, Journal of Family Business Strategy* and *Journal of Family Business Management*. This evolution is also well represented in Figure 2, where earlier topics are visually marked in blue and most recent ones in yellow.

Early on, most of family business research was focused on the basic elements and definitional characteristics of family business. The aim was to introduce family firms as organizations worth been investigated and to show that peculiar characteristics define this type of organization. In so doing, scholars focused on topics such as family involvement in the ownership and/or in the management (e.g., Kellermanns et al., 2008), family influence (e.g., Klein et al., 2005), values (e.g., García-Álvarez & López-Sintas, 2001), identity (e.g., Zellweger et al., 2010), trust (e.g., LaChapelle & Barnes, 1998), and social capital (e.g., Arregle

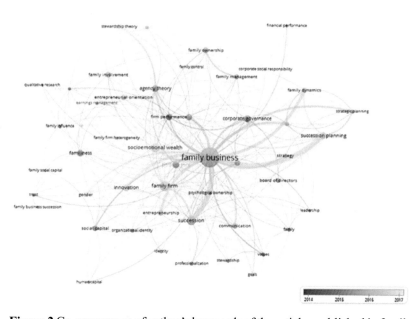

Figure 2 Co-occurrence of author's keywords of the articles published in family business journals and their evolution.

Source: Rovelli et al. (2021)

et al., 2007), and linked these elements to important outcomes, such as firm performance (e.g., Sciascia & Mazzola, 2008). As the field developed, scholarly interests broadened to encompass family firms' drivers of behaviors and strategies. In this regard, the two most recurrent topics are SEW (e.g., Berrone et al., 2012; Gomez-Mejia et al., 2007) and succession planning (e.g., Gilding et al., 2015; Molly et al., 2010). Finally, family business research has recently started to investigate broader topics in the general management literature, such as innovation (e.g., De Massis et al., 2018b; Diéguez-Soto et al., 2016), gender issues (e.g., Akhmedova et al., 2020; Chadwick & Dawson, 2018), and CSR (e.g., Cabeza-García et al., 2017; Cruz et al., 2019), among many others.

Half of the papers in our sample (495 articles, 54.52 percent) do not mention a specific theory in their title or abstract. This suggests that the family business field is still driven for the most part by topics and interesting phenomena, rather than theoretical advancement. The field, however, is rapidly moving toward a deeper integration of theories borrowed from other disciplines as well as growing effort to build and develop original theories based on its unique context. Figure 3 shows a zoom in on the theoretical lenses adopted so far by family business scholars (considering theories mentioned in at least four papers in the sample we analyzed). According to their title or abstract, scholars made a relatively limited use of theories in the emergence phase – nine theories out of the sixteen represented in the figure. The predominant theoretical lens used in this phase is agency theory, which appears in thirty-three articles, followed by the RBV (eleven papers) and stewardship theory (ten papers); the remaining theories are mentioned by three or less articles. Moreover, it is worth mentioning that neither of the theories listed in the figure appears in the papers published between 1995 and 1999.

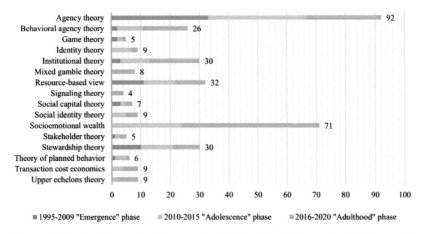

Figure 3 Trend of theoretical lenses adopted by at least five papers in the sample

The number of theories adopted by family business scholars has increased in the adolescence phase. This phase is marked by the introduction of the SEW perspective, which has been used by twenty-four articles in that time frame. This perspective is accompanied by agency theory (thirty-four papers), stewardship theory (eleven), RBV (eleven), and institutional theory (ten). The remaining theories are mentioned by less than ten papers published in this period (e.g., behavioral agency theory, identity theory). Finally, the adulthood phase is dominated by the SEW perspective, which is mentioned by forty-seven papers: agency theory (twenty-five papers), institutional theory (seventeen), behavioral agency theory (fifteen), and RBV (ten) follow. Worth mentioning are also stewardship theory (cited in nine abstracts), mixed-gamble theory (seven), and upper echelons theory (seven).

Considering the three phases altogether, the theoretical lenses (Figure 3) used most frequently are agency theory – mentioned by ninety-two papers – and the SEW perspective – mentioned by seventy-one articles. Much less predominant but still frequent are four other theories: RBV (thirty-two), institutional theory (thirty), stewardship theory (thirty), and behavioral agency theory (twenty-six).

After looking at the evolution of the family business research field, we now move to an exploration of the extant literature from a different perspective – the one of top-tier management journals. We specifically look at family business papers published in these journals to assess what conversations about family business have moved outside the specialist domain. This is important to establish common theoretical areas of interest and potential convergences in empirical domains.

3 Family Business Contributions in Management Journals

To begin to understand how research on family businesses has intersected conversations in generalist, rather than specialist, management journals, we conducted an analysis of "family business" publications in high-quality management journals. These are journals listed in the FT50 and classified as ABS 4/4*. This analysis was driven by the following questions: *When family business papers are published in nonspecialist outlets? What type of theoretical contributions do they make?* We know that every academic journal requires a strong contribution to theory to be granted publication. Hence, studies of family businesses need to offer insights that go beyond extending knowledge of family firms as an empirical context. Our search covered the following journals: *Academy of Management Journal, Academy of Management Review, Administrative Science Quarterly, Journal of Management, Journal of Management Studies, Organization Science, Organization Studies.* This selection resulted in seventy-six articles published in the time frame 1998–2021. To examine the papers and their contributions, we applied a framework developed by Neubaum and Micelotta (2021) that classifies contributions based on two dimensions: contextual orientation and target audience. In the following sections, we present the framework and use it to explain how family business research has made important contributions in management journals.

3.1 Types of Theoretical Contributions

The 2×2 matrix looks at two dimensions that help position a paper into the literature and define its potential contribution to a body of work: (1) the *contextual orientation* of the researcher and (2) the *target audience* to which the contribution is intended. We discuss these two dimensions before considering how their intersection reveals four different types of papers in the family business domain (Table 3).

3.1.1 Contextual Orientation

The idea of contextual orientation was developed by Blair and Hunt (1986) to "get inside the head of management researchers" (p. 147) and appreciate differences in their "cognitive styles" (p. 147). Contextual orientation is defined as "the basic way in which a management researcher thinks about the phenomenon he or she is studying" (p. 148). Seen as a continuum, contextual orientation spans between a "context-free" orientation and a "context-specific" orientation.

A *context-free orientation* (or theory-specific orientation) is the approach of a researcher whose research interest primarily lies in a theoretical perspective (e.g., institutional theory or agency theory). The research focus is primarily on the key constructs and variables underpinning the theory (e.g., legitimacy in the case of institutional theory, agency costs in the case of agency theory). The contribution of the researcher is to advance the theory through conceptual and empirical research. Relatively less emphasis is placed on the contexts or settings that can be used to empirically test the predictions of the theory (quantitative research) or to examine its underpinning processes or mechanisms (qualitative research). From the vantage point of the researcher, it is not relevant whether empirical studies are conducted in nonprofit organizations or large conglomerates, in health care or professional service firms. The researcher may develop in-depth knowledge about these settings, if engaging in qualitative research, for example. However, the primary contribution is to the theory itself.

A *context-specific orientation* is the approach of a researcher whose interest lies in developing in-depth knowledge about a specific type of organization, such as family business, health care, or professional service firms or nonprofits. The goal of the researcher is to understand its specific challenges and behaviors.

Table 3 Types of FB papers and their contributions

		WHICH CONVERSATION IS THE CONTRIBUTION TO?	
		Specialist contribution to FB audience	Generalist contribution to MGMT audience
WHICH CONVERSATION IS THE CONTRIBUTION TO?	Context specific	**EMBEDDED** ✓ Draws on ad hoc theoretical frameworks to reveal and explain strategies and behaviors in family firms ✓ Offers theoretical insights that, in the aggregate, can help develop theories unique to family businesses	**CHALLENGER** ✓ Questions the assumptions and predictions of an existing theory in the context of family firms ✓ Establishes boundary conditions for an existing theory by considering family ownership ✓ Supports the development of unique FB theories (e.g., socioemotional wealth)
	Context free or theory specific	**INTEGRATIVE** ✓ Applies a theoretical concept or perspective from another field to the family business domain to generate theory ✓ Extends the theoretical breadth of existing FB research by connecting with adjacent theories and closing the theoretical loop	**GENERALIZED** ✓ Addresses questions and extends knowledge in a nonfamily theoretical domain ✓ Utilizes the "family firm" as an ideal setting to isolate and study a phenomenon ✓ Offers some implications for family business scholarship

There is less emphasis on the theoretical tools that will be used to achieve this goal, because the array of phenomena involving these organizations is wide and multifaceted. Hence, context-specific research is often theory-agnostic: a researcher may use different theoretical lenses depending on which lens is the most useful to address the specific research question at hand. Insights from a specific type of organization are likely to tackle important problems that managers face and to be more easily translated into "best practices" that consultants working in these organizations can use. Not surprisingly, this approach was dominant in the early stages of family business research, when the primary interest was to capture the unique features and challenges of this type of organization. As the field has evolved, however, the push to integrate family business research into existing theoretical domains has grown stronger.

3.1.2 Target Audience

A second aspect of theoretical contribution is *to what* exactly a scholar seeks to contribute. A contribution is often associated with the idea of "joining a conversation" among scholars (Huff, 1999). Indeed, research is conducted by drawing on prior work and "standing on the shoulders of giants." So, the question becomes: *To what conversation is your paper contributing? What audience is being targeted? And what body of knowledge are you going to extend or challenge?* To simplify, we can think of two options for family business researchers: a specialist contribution to FB scholarship or a generalist contribution to management (MGMT) scholarship.

First, a scholar may want to pursue research that advances specific knowledge about family firms. The goal is to join a relatively specialized conversation, provide rich insights into organizational processes and mechanisms that are relevant for this type of organization, or to test hypotheses about variables that impact their behaviors and outcomes. The knowledge generated by these studies is typically domain-specific, and generalization to other settings is therefore relatively more difficult. These contributions are particularly welcome in management journals that are friendly to the family business research field (e.g., *Entrepreneurship: Theory and Practice*) and, more generally, journals that are interested in advancing knowledge about family firms. If the contribution to this field of research is clear, it is unlikely that findings will be expected to generalize their findings to other types of organization.

Alternatively, a scholar may think of contributing to a broader conversation in management studies. For example, advancing a theoretical debate (e.g., what drives companies to internalize pressures to engage in socially responsible behaviors? – Berrone et al., 2010), extending a theory by testing moderators or mediators (e.g., how does family ownership affect the prediction of behavioral theory on R&D

investments? – Chrisman & Patel, 2012), or enriching a field of study such as networks (e.g., how do actors in a multiplex relationship – one crossing multiple domains – struggle to transition into new roles in one domain without disrupting existing interactions and the role hierarchy in another? – Li & Piezunka, 2020). In this scenario, the family business context provides an excellent setting to address calls for *contextualization* of management research. In several disciplines, there has been increasing disquiet over the excessive focus of empirical research on theoretical development at the expense of understanding the context in which theories are being elaborated. For instance, scholars in OB – a large subdiscipline of management – recognize that "the variety of contexts OB researchers encounter require them to pay special attention when exporting scientific constructs and research methodologies" (Rousseau & Fried, 2001, p. 2). Along the same line, entrepreneurship scholars advocate for more attention to the context of entrepreneurial efforts, to avoid building theories only based on the "decontextualized 'standard model' of entrepreneurship of the Silicon Valley" (Welter et al., 2019, p. 320). Importantly, there is a strong push to create "indigenous theories," research that does not aim to test an existing theory but to derive new theories of the phenomena in their specific contexts (Tsui, 2004, p. 501). For family business scholarship, the push for contextualization brings tremendous opportunities to use the distinctive context of family firms to develop highly contextualized theories, and thereby provide a contribution to management scholarship. Typically, these contributions can be found in generalist management journals (e.g., *Academy of Management Journal, Administrative Science Quarterly, Organization Studies*). If the contribution is based on a family business setting, findings are expected to be generalizable to other types of organization.

When these two dimensions are considered together, four types of family business papers emerge: (1) embedded; (2) integrative; (3) challenger; and (4) generalized (Figure 4). In the following, we provide a definition of each of these types and present an overview of the contributions of family business research pertaining to each type.

3.2 Categorization of Family Business Research Based on Contribution

To start with, we report in Table 4 information about the seventy-seven "family business" papers published in high-quality management journals that we examined. We categorized these articles based on the quadrants of the matrix. Although classifications are subjective, what we are most interested in is to try to explain the type of contextual orientation and target audience of these papers, and therefore the type of theoretical conversations they advance.

Table 4 FB papers published in top management journals

Author(s)	Title	Year	Journal	Type	Theory(ies)	Approach	Sample
Chirico F., Welsh D. H. B., Ireland R. D., Sieger P.	Family versus nonfamily firm franchisors: Behavioral and performance differences	2021	*Journal of Management Studies*	Embedded	Resource-based view	Quantitative	Family and nonfamily firms
Fang H., Memili E., Chrisman J. J., Tang L.	Narrow framing and risk preferences in family and nonfamily firms	2021	*Journal of Management Studies*	Embedded	Prospect theory	Quantitative	Family and nonfamily firms
De Massis A., Eddleston K. A., Rovelli P.	Entrepreneurial by design: How organizational design affects family and nonfamily firms' opportunity exploitation	2021	*Journal of Management Studies*	Embedded	Organizational design perspective	Quantitative	Family and nonfamily firms

Authors	Title	Year	Journal		Theory	Method	Context
Prügl, R., & Spitzley, D. I.	Responding to digital transformation by external corporate venturing: An enterprising family identity and communication patterns perspective	2021	*Journal of Management Studies*	Embedded	Identity and communication patterns	Quantitative	Family firms
Raitis J., Sasaki I., Kotlar J.	System-spanning values work and entrepreneurial growth in family firms	2021	*Journal of Management Studies*	Embedded	Family system theory	Qualitative	Family firms
Ramírez-Pasillas M., Lundberg H., Nordqvist M.	Next generation external venturing practices in family-owned businesses	2021	*Journal of Management Studies*	Embedded	Entrepreneurship as Practice	Qualitative	Family firms
Huang X., Chen L., Xu E., Lu F., Tam K. -C.	Shadow of the prince: Parent-incumbents' coercive control over child-successors in family organizations	2020	*Administrative Science Quarterly*	Embedded	SEW; Theory of the double-bind paradox	Quantitative	Family firms

Table 4 (cont.)

Author(s)	Title	Year	Journal	Type	Theory(ies)	Approach	Sample
Gu Q., Lu J. W., Chung C. -N.	Incentive or disincentive? A SEW explanation of new industry entry in family business groups	2019	*Journal of Management*	Embedded	SEW	Quantitative	Family firms
Nason R., Mazzelli A., Carney M.	The ties that unbind: Socialization and business-owning family reference point shift	2019	*Academy of Management Review*	Embedded	Behavioral agency theory; SEW	Conceptual	Family firms
Kim H, Hoskisson R. E., Zyung J. D.	Socioemotional favoritism: Evidence from foreign divestitures in family multinationals	2019	*Organization Studies*	Embedded	SEW	Quantitative	Family firms
Vandekerkhof P., Steijvers T., Hendriks W., Voordeckers W.	Socioemotional wealth separation and decision-making quality in family firm TMTs: The moderating role of psychological safety	2018	*Journal of Management Studies*	Embedded	SEW	Quantitative	Family firms

Authors	Title	Year	Journal		Topic	Method	Sample
Zattoni A., Gnan L., Huse M.	Does family involvement influence firm performance? Exploring the mediating effects of board processes and tasks	2015	*Journal of Management*	Embedded	Corporate governance: Boards	Quantitative	Family and nonfamily firms
Minichilli A., Nordqvist M., Corbetta G., Amore M. D.	CEO succession mechanisms, organizational context, and performance: A socioemotional wealth perspective on family-controlled firms	2014	*Journal of Management Studies*	Embedded	SEW	Quantitative	Family firms
König A., Kammerlander N., Enders A.	The family innovator's dilemma: how family influence affects the adoption of discontinuous technologies by incumbent firms	2013	*Academy of Management Review*	Embedded	Discontinuous technological change	Conceptual	Family firms

Table 4 (cont.)

Author(s)	Title	Year	Journal	Type	Theory(ies)	Approach	Sample
Miller D., Le Breton-Miller I., Lester R. H.	Family firm governance, strategic conformity, and performance: institutional versus strategic perspectives	2013	*Organization Science*	Embedded	Institutional theory; SEW	Quantitative	Family and nonfamily firms
Zellweger T. M., Kellermanns F. W., Chrisman J. J., Chua J. H.	Family control and family firm valuation by family CEOs: The importance of intentions for transgenerational control	2012	*Organization Science*	Embedded	Prospect theory	Quantitative	Family firms
Gomez-Mejia L. R., Makri M., Kintana M. L.	Diversification decisions in family-controlled firms	2010	*Journal of Management Studies*	Embedded	Behavioral agency theory; SEW	Quantitative	Family and nonfamily firms
Ling Y., Kellermanns F. W.	The effects of family firm-specific sources of TMT diversity: The moderating role of information exchange frequency	2010	*Journal of Management Studies*	Embedded	Team process; Upper echelons theory	Quantitative	Family firms

Authors	Year	Journal		Theory	Method	Sample
Yoshikawa T., Rasheed A. A.	2010	*Journal of Management Studies*	Embedded	Agency theory	Quantitative	Family firms
Figener M. K.	2010	*Journal of Management Studies*	Embedded	Agency theory	Quantitative	Family and nonfamily firms
Minichilli A., Corbetta G., MacMillan I. C.	2010	*Journal of Management Studies*	Embedded	Agency theory; Upper echelons theory	Quantitative	Family firms
Peng M. W., Jiang Y.	2010	*Journal of Management Studies*	Embedded	Agency theory; Institution-based view; Resource-based view	Quantitative	Family firms

Title column entries (by author):
- Yoshikawa T., Rasheed A. A. — Family control and ownership monitoring in family-controlled firms in Japan
- Figener M. K. — Locus of ownership and family involvement in small private firms
- Minichilli A., Corbetta G., MacMillan I. C. — Top management teams in family-controlled companies: "Familiness," "faultlines," and their impact on financial performance
- Peng M. W., Jiang Y. — Institutions behind family ownership and control in large firms

Table 4 (cont.)

Author(s)	Title	Year	Journal	Type	Theory(ies)	Approach	Sample
Zahra S. A.	Harvesting family firms' organizational social capital: A relational perspective	2010	*Journal of Management Studies*	Embedded	Organizational Social Capital (OSC)	Quantitative	Family and nonfamily firms
Miller D., Le Breton-Miller I., Scholnick B.	Stewardship versus stagnation: An empirical comparison of small family and nonfamily businesses	2008	*Journal of Management Studies*	Embedded	Stewardship theory	Quantitative	Family and nonfamily firms
Tsui-Auch L. S.	The professionally managed family-ruled enterprise: Ethnic Chinese business in Singapore	2004	*Journal of Management Studies*	Embedded	Institutional theory	Qualitative	Family firms
Davies H., Ma C.	Strategic choice and the nature of the Chinese family business: An exploratory study of the Hong Kong watch industry	2003	*Organization Studies*	Embedded	Strategic choice and institutional characteristics	Quantitative	Family firms

Authors	Title	Year	Journal		Theory	Method	Firm type
Tsui-Auch L. S., Lee Y. -J.	The state matters: Management models of Singaporean Chinese and Korean business groups	2003	Organization Studies	Embedded	Business systems and institutions	Qualitative	Family firms
Lee K. S., Lim G. H., Lim W. S.	Family business succession: Appropriation risk and choice of successor	2003	Academy of Management Review	Embedded	Game theory	Conceptual	Family firms
Rademakers M. F. L.	Market organization in Indonesia: Javanese and Chinese family business in the jamu industry	1998	Organization Studies	Embedded	Business system approach	Qualitative	Family firms
Ge J., Micelotta E.	When does the family matter? Institutional pressures and corporate philanthropy in China	2019	Organization Studies	Integrative	Institutional theory	Quantitative	Family and nonfamily firms

Table 4 (cont.)

Author(s)	Title	Year	Journal	Type	Theory(ies)	Approach	Sample
Sasaki I., Ravasi D., Micelotta E.	Family firms as institutions: Cultural reproduction and status maintenance among multi-centenary shinise in Kyoto	2019	*Organization Studies*	Integrative	Institutional theory	Qualitative	Family firms
Vincent Ponroy J., Lê P., Pradies C.	In a family way? A model of family firm identity maintenance by nonfamily members	2019	*Organization Studies*	Integrative	Organizational identity theory	Qualitative	Family firms
Lingo E.L., Elmes M.B.	Institutional preservation work at a family business in crisis: Micro-processes, emotions, and nonfamily members	2019	*Organization Studies*	Integrative	Institutional theory	Qualitative	Family firms

Authors	Title	Year	Journal		Theory		
Gomez-Mejia L. R., Neacsu I., Martin G.	CEO risk-taking and SEW: the behavioral agency model, family control, and CEO option wealth	2019	*Journal of Management*	Integrative	Behavioral agency theory; SEW	Quantitative	Family and nonfamily firms
Bird M., Zellweger T.	Relational embeddedness and firm growth: Comparing spousal and sibling entrepreneurs	2018	*Organization Science*	Integrative	Relational embeddedness and growth theory	Quantitative	Family and nonfamily firms
Gomez-Mejia L. R., Patel P. C., Zellweger T.M.	In the horns of the dilemma: SEW, financial wealth, and acquisitions in family firms	2018	*Journal of Management*	Integrative	Behavioral agency theory; Mixed-gamble theory; SEW	Quantitative	Family and nonfamily firms
Kotlar J., Signori A., De Massis A., Vismara S.	Financial wealth, SEW, and IPO underpricing in family firms: A two-stage gamble model	2018	*Academy of Management Journal*	Integrative	Behavioral agency theory; prospect theory (mixed gamble)	Quantitative	Family and nonfamily firms
Neckebrouck J., Schulze W., Zellweger T.	Are family firms good employers?	2018	*Academy of Management Journal*	Integrative	Agency theory; Stewardship theory	Quantitative	Family and nonfamily firms

Table 4 (cont.)

Author(s)	Title	Year	Journal	Type	Theory(ies)	Approach	Sample
Strike V. M., Rerup C.	Mediated sensemaking	2016	*Academy of Management Journal*	Integrative	Sensemaking theory; adaptive mediation	Qualitative	Family firms
Cannella A. A., Jr., Jones C. D., Withers M. C.	Family- versus lone founder-controlled public corporations: Social identity theory and boards of directors	2015	*Academy of Management Journal*	Integrative	Social identity theory; Boards	Quantitative	Family and nonfamily firms
Miller D., Le Breton-Miller I., Minichilli A., Corbetta G., Pittino D.	When do nonfamily CEOs outperform in family firms? Agency and behavioral agency perspectives	2014	*Journal of Management Studies*	Integrative	Agency theory; Behavioral agency theory	Quantitative	Family firms
Deephouse D. L., Jaskiewicz P.	Do family firms have better reputations than nonfamily firms? An integration of SEW and social identity theories	2013	*Journal of Management Studies*	Integrative	SEW; Social identity theory	Quantitative	Family and nonfamily firms

Authors	Title	Year	Journal		Theory		
Luo X. R., Chung C.-N.	Filling or abusing the institutional void? Ownership and management control of public family businesses in an emerging market	2013	*Organization Science*	Integrative	Agency theory; Institutional economics	Quantitative	Family and nonfamily firms
Herrero I.	Agency costs, family ties, and firm efficiency	2011	*Journal of Management*	Integrative	Agency theory	Quantitative	Family and nonfamily firms
Le Breton-Miller I., Miller D., Lester R. H.	Stewardship or agency? A social embeddedness reconciliation of conduct and performance in public family businesses	2011	*Organization Science*	Integrative	Agency theory; Stewardship theory	Quantitative	Family and nonfamily firms
Miller D., Le Breton-Miller I., Lester R. H.	Family and lone founder ownership and strategic behavior: Social context, identity, and institutional logics	2011	*Journal of Management Studies*	Integrative	Agency theory; Identity and social theory; Institutional logics	Quantitative	Family and nonfamily firms

Table 4 (cont.)

Author(s)	Title	Year	Journal	Type	Theory(ies)	Approach	Sample
Eddleston K. A., Kellermanns F. W., Sarathy R.	Resource configuration in family firms: Linking resources, strategic planning, and technological opportunities to performance	2008	*Journal of Management Studies*	Integrative	RBV; Stewardship theory	Quantitative	Family firms
Wu W. -P.	Dimensions of social capital and firm competitiveness improvement: The mediating role of information sharing	2008	*Journal of Management Studies*	Integrative	Social capital theory	Quantitative	Family firms
Lubatkin M. H., Ling Y., Schulze W. S.	An organizational justice-based view of self-control and agency costs in family firms	2007	*Journal of Management Studies*	Integrative	Agency theory; Behavioral agency theory; Justice theory	Conceptual	Family firms

Authors	Title	Year	Journal	Type	Theory	Method	Sample
Gomez-Mejia L. R., Larraza-Kintana M., Makri M.	The determinants of executive compensation in family-controlled public corporations	2003	*Academy of Management Journal*	Integrative	Agency theory	Quantitative	Family firms
Schulze W. S., Lubatkin M. H., Dino R. N.	Exploring the agency consequences of ownership dispersion among the directors of private family firms	2003	*Academy of Management Journal*	Integrative	Agency theory	Quantitative	Family firms
Schulze W. S., Lubatkin M. H., Dino R. N., Buchholtz A. K.	Agency relationships in family firms: theory and evidence	2001	*Organization Science*	Integrative	Agency theory; Economic theory of the household	Quantitative	Family firms
Chirico F., Gómez-Mejia L. R., Hellerstedt K., Withers M., Nordqvist M.	To merge, sell, or liquidate? SEW, family control, and the choice of business exit	2020	*Journal of Management*	Challenger	Behavioral agency theory; SEW	Quantitative	Family and nonfamily firms

Table 4 (cont.)

Author(s)	Title	Year	Journal	Type	Theory(ies)	Approach	Sample
Jaskiewicz P., Block J. H., Miller D., Combs J. G.	Founder versus family owners' impact on pay dispersion among non-CEO top managers: Implications for firm performance	2017	*Journal of Management*	Challenger	Agency theory; Social comparison theory	Quantitative	Family and nonfamily firms
Strike V. M., Berrone P., Sapp S. G., Congiu L.	A SEW approach to CEO career horizons in family firms	2015	*Journal of Management Studies*	Challenger	Agency theory; SEW	Quantitative	Family and nonfamily firms
Chrisman J. J., Patel P. C.	Variations in R&D investments of family and nonfamily firms: Behavioral agency and myopic loss aversion perspectives	2012	*Academy of Management Journal*	Challenger	Behavioral agency model; Prospect theory	Quantitative	Family and nonfamily firms
Berrone P., Cruz C., Gomez-Mejia L. R., Larraza-Kintana M.	SEW and corporate responses to institutional pressures: Do family-controlled firms pollute less?	2010	*Administrative Science Quarterly*	Challenger	SEW; Institutional theory	Quantitative	Family and nonfamily firms

Authors	Title	Year	Journal	Type	Theory	Method	Firms
Gómez-Mejía L. R., Haynes K. T., Núñez-Nickel M., Jacobson K. J. L., Moyano-Fuentes J.	SEW and business risks in family-controlled firms: Evidence from Spanish olive oil mills	2007	*Administrative Science Quarterly*	Challenger	SEW; Behavioral agency theory	Quantitative	Family firms
Anderson R. C., Reeb D. M.	Board composition: Balancing family influence in S&P 500 firms	2004	*Administrative Science Quarterly*	Challenger	Agency theory; Stewardship theory	Quantitative	Family and nonfamily firms
Gomez-Mejía L. R., Nuñez-Nickel M., Gutierrez I.	The role of family ties in agency contracts	2001	*Academy of Management Journal*	Challenger	Agency theory	Quantitative	Family and nonfamily firms
Byrne J., Radu-Lefebvre M., Fattoum S., Balachandra L.	Gender gymnastics in CEO succession: Masculinities, femininities, and legitimacy	2019	*Organization Studies*	Generalized	CEO succession and doing gender	Qualitative	Family firms
Eddleston K. A., Banalieva E. R., Verbeke A.	The bribery paradox in transition economies and the enactment of "new normal" business environments	2020	*Journal of Management Studies*	Generalized	Corruption and sensemaking theory	Quantitative	Family and nonfamily firms

Table 4 (cont.)

Author(s)	Title	Year	Journal	Type	Theory(ies)	Approach	Sample
Li J. B., Piezunka H.	The uniplex third: Enabling single-domain role transitions in multiplex relationships	2020	*Administrative Science Quarterly*	Generalized	Multiplex relationships and role transitions	Qualitative	Family firms
Luo X. R., Jeong Y. -C., Chung C. -N.	In the eye of the beholder: Global analysts' coverage of family firms in an emerging market	2019	*Journal of Management*	Generalized	Agency theory; Institutional logics	Quantitative	Family and nonfamily firms
Schiehll E., Lewellyn K. B., Muller-Kahle M. I.	Pilot, pivot, and advisory boards: The role of governance configurations in innovation commitment	2018	*Organization Studies*	Generalized	Agency theory; Resource dependence theory	Qualitative	Family and nonfamily firms

Authors	Title	Year	Journal		Theory	Method	Firm type
Richards M., Zellweger T., Gond J.-P.	Maintaining moral legitimacy through worlds and words: An explanation of firms' investment in sustainability certification	2017	*Journal of Management Studies*	Generalized	French pragmatist sociology	Quantitative	Family and nonfamily firms
Haynes K. T., Hitt M. A., Campbell J. T.	The dark side of leadership: Toward a mid-range theory of hubris and greed in entrepreneurial contexts	2015	*Journal of Management Studies*	Generalized	Greed, hubris, leadership; SEW	Conceptual	Family and nonfamily firms
Patel P. C., Cooper D.	Structural power equality between family and nonfamily TMT members and the performance of family firms	2014	*Academy of Management Journal*	Generalized	Upper echelon; structural power	Quantitative	Family firms

Table 4 (cont.)

Author(s)	Title	Year	Journal	Type	Theory(ies)	Approach	Sample
Petriglieri G., Stein M.	The unwanted self: Projective identification in leaders' identity work	2012	*Organization Studies*	Generalized	Identity theory	Qualitative	Family firms
Cruz C. C., Gómez-Mejia L. R., Becerra M.	Perceptions of benevolence and the design of agency contracts: CEO-TMT relationships in family firms	2010	*Academy of Management Journal*	Generalized	Agency theory	Quantitative	Family firms
Chung C. -N., Luo X.	Institutional logics or agency costs: The influence of corporate governance models on business group restructuring in emerging economies	2008	*Organization Science*	Generalized	Agency theory; Institutional logics	Quantitative	Family and nonfamily firms

Author	Title	Year	Journal		Theory	Method	Firm type
Hicheon K., Heechun K., Peggy M. L.	Ownership structure and the relationship between financial slack and R&D investments: evidence from Korean firms	2008	*Organization Science*	Generalized	Agency theory	Quantitative	Family and nonfamily firms
Arregle J. -L., Hitt M. A., Sirmon D. G., Very P.	The development of organizational social capital: Attributes of family firms	2007	*Journal of Management Studies*	Generalized	Social capital theory	Conceptual	Family firms
Carr C.	Are German, Japanese and Anglo-Saxon strategic decision styles still divergent in the context of globalization?	2005	*Journal of Management Studies*	Generalized	Strategic decisions; globalization	Quantitative	Family and nonfamily firms
Tsui-Auch L. S.	Unpacking regional ethnicity and the strength of ties in shaping ethnic entrepreneurship	2005	*Organization Studies*	Generalized	Ethnic entrepreneurship	Qualitative	Family and nonfamily firms

Table 4 (cont.)

Author(s)	Title	Year	Journal	Type	Theory(ies)	Approach	Sample
Ainsworth S., Cox J. W.	Families divided: Culture and control in small family business	2003	*Organization Studies*	Generalized	Critical theory; organizational control	Qualitative	Family firms
Carney M., Gedajlovic E.	The coupling of ownership and control and the allocation of financial resources: Evidence from Hong Kong	2002	*Journal of Management Studies*	Generalized	Corporate governance; forms of capitalism	Quantitative	Family firms

3.2.1 Embedded

This is a type of FB paper where the focus is context-specific (i.e., family firms as a specific type of organization), and the goal of the authors is to advance specialist knowledge about family firms. When positioning their papers, the authors assume that the audience is knowledgeable about the domain of family firms, and the originality and novelty of the paper need to reside into expanding the conversation into new domains and providing new insights about strategies and behaviors of family businesses. Most embedded FB papers are published in specialist journals such as *Family Business Review* and *Journal of Family Business Strategy*. However, an increasing number of generalist management journals are becoming "hosts" for family business research, typically in the form of special issues (e.g., *Journal of Management Studies*; *Organization Studies*). The sensitivity and openness of management journals to family business research depends on editorial choices and the scope of the journal.

Embedded FB papers published in top management journals are typically collections of articles aimed at advancing context-specific knowledge in the family business domain. Authors draw on ad hoc theoretical frameworks to reveal and explain processes and outcomes, as well as new strategies and behaviors, observed in family firms (e.g., De Massis et al., 2021; König et al., 2013; Minichilli et al., 2014; Raitis et al., 2021; Ramírez-Pasillas et al., 2021). Within this category, most studies focus on emerging topics in other fields (e.g., corporate entrepreneurship (CE)) and contribute to the literature by providing new insights on how this topic applies in the peculiar business context of family firms. For instance, in this set of papers are included the articles published in two special issues of the *Journal of Management Studies*. The first one, published in 2010, was titled "The family and enterprise: Unpacking the connections." The goal was to motivate theoretically grounded research that could explain "the prevalence, prominence, or even existence" of the family enterprise as an "economic institution" (Schulze & Gedajlovic, 2010, p. 191). As the editors noted, research about family business at the time was still "in its infancy" and the "diversity of theories and perspectives represented in the developing literature portray a cluttered and conflicted landscape." The published papers draw on a wide array of theoretical frameworks, from economics, management, and sociology. Along the same line, a second *Journal of Management Studies* Special Issue published in 2021 focused on "Corporate entrepreneurship and family business: Learning across disciplines." Once again, this is a conversation started by several authors on CE in the family business context (Chirico et al., 2021; De Massis et al., 2021;

Ramírez-Pasillas et al., 2021). Papers focused on the process of CE in family firms and, once again, "theories applied include, among others, the resource-based view, contingency theory, and family system theory – again mirroring the broad perspective required to advance the field" (Minola et al., 2021, p. 5).

Where Is Organization Theory? As evident in Table 4, theoretical frameworks in OT are not well represented in this category of papers. We have already discussed that FB research has been deeply influenced by strategic and economic frameworks (e.g., behavioral agency theory, RBV), which align well with the interest in corporate governance and decision-making in family firms. These frameworks also tie relatively directly with the SEW perspective, which is highly influential in FB research. In comparison, there is a striking absence of classical organization theories (e.g., resource dependency, population ecology) and a selective use of institutional theory, mostly to account for institutional influences on family businesses in countries with very different institutional regimes from Europe or North America. Perhaps not surprisingly, most of the papers are quantitative (seventeen), whereas a small number (five) develop theory qualitatively or conceptually (three).

New Theories. Interestingly, a couple of papers reveal the potential of developing theory that is highly and deeply embedded in the FB domain. Three studies attempt to provide new insights about family businesses, by developing (new) theories specific to the family businesses field of research (e.g., Nason et al., 2019). Lee et al. (2003) offered an Academy of Management Review note where they provide an economic rationale to succession in FB based on transaction cost economics (TCE). To do so, they integrate research on managerial succession, family businesses, and TCE. The work by König et al. (2013) also tackles a perennial issue: discontinuous technological change by incumbents. It shows how theories of organizational change in family firms need to consider that family influence shifts organizational constraints, with the result that "innovators in family-influenced companies face fundamentally different dilemmas." Finally, the study by Nason et al. (2019) explains how specific social interactions can alter the collective knowledge structures of business-owning families by changing the way they interpret and filter their environment through reference points. In doing so, they introduce a new theory about socialization and socio-cognitive processes in family firms.

3.2.2 Integrative

This second type of paper is also intended for a specialist family business audience, but the contextual orientation of the authors is theory specific.

Scholars are typically well versed in a theoretical perspective and use it to address research questions that involve family business. These papers generate novel and original insights about family businesses by integrating theoretical frameworks and concepts that have not been extensively utilized or applied to this specialized domain. In other words, integrative studies connect a theoretical concept or perspective from another field and integrate it into the family business domain (e.g., Ge & Micelotta, 2019; Strike & Rerup, 2016). By doing so, they extend the theoretical breadth of existing family business research by connecting it with adjacent theories and therefore closing the theoretical loop (e.g., Cannella Jr. et al., 2015; Le Breton-Miller et al., 2011; Miller et al., 2011; Minichilli et al., 2010).

For example, this was the main goal of the *Organization Studies* special issues published in 2019 on "Coupling family business research with organization studies." As the editors suggested, family firms are not extensively studied by organizational scholars and there are several opportunities to advance both fields. In their introduction to the Special Issue, they highlight five areas that are core in defining features of family firms – ownership, management and governance, transgenerational intention, generational involvement, and perceived identity – and can be linked to organization studies relatively directly (Salvato et al., 2019).

Most of the studies within this category *integrate* two or more existing theoretical approaches that originated outside the family business field of research to explain specific behaviors or to provide new insights about family firms. For instance, Cannella Jr. et al. (2015) integrate social identity and organizational identification with theories of ownership to understand differences between family firms and lone founder firms, and how these differences reflect in the board structure of these organizations. Similarly, Le Breton-Miller et al. (2011) reconcile two traditionally contradictory theoretical perspective – that is, stewardship and agency theory – to explain the degree of embeddedness of the firm with the family and thus how much it identifies with the family's interests.

Other studies within the integrative category generate their contributions by drawing upon existing theories and adapt the theoretical framework to fit some peculiarities of family firms. The proposed novelty and originality of the paper resides in looking at a phenomenon in family business through the lens of an existing theoretical approach that has been developed in other streams of research and not extensively utilized or applied to family firms. The goal is to shed light on a phenomenon of interest for family firms through insights that are derived from the theoretical understanding that this lens provides. However, by using a novel theoretical lens, these works are not only able to contribute to the family business literature, but also to extend the primary theoretical perspective they draw on. For instance, Strike and Rerup (2016) theorized the concept of mediated sensemaking, which is particularly relevant in FB due to the heavy reliance on trusted advisors. The paper advances research on trusted advisors in family firms (a very specific research interest). However, by drawing upon sensemaking theory, the authors revealed the importance of mediated sense-making, which is highly relevant for a broader audience.

Where Is Organization Theory? In analyzing papers that belong to the integrative type, we were once again perplexed by the relative dearth of OT frameworks in the FB literature published in generalist management journals. In line with the review conducted by Odom et al. (2019) on the most cited papers in the FB literature (2009–13), the most prevalent theoretical frameworks are agency theory, RBV, stewardship theory, SEW, and institutional theory. Institutional theory is highly represented in the *Organization Studies* Special Issue, where three papers used this perspective (Ge & Micelotta, 2019; Lingo & Elmes, 2019; Sasaki et al., 2019). The institutional perspective is used in different ways: to explain conforming behaviors in corporate philanthropy in Chinese firms and differentiate those choices from reputational concerns (Ge & Micelotta, 2019), in the Selznick perspective to explain the longevity and status maintenance of centenary firms that surge to the status of "institutions" (Sasaki et al., 2019), in the agentic work perspective to explain how low-power individuals (i.e., nonfamily members) can come to identify with an organization and act as agents of institutional preservation for the organization (Lingo & Elmes, 2019). Other organization theories that resonated with authors of integrative papers are the institutional logics perspective combined with identity theory (Miller et al., 2011), sensemaking (Strike & Rerup, 2016), identity maintenance (Ponroy et al., 2019), and social identity theory (Cannella Jr. et al., 2015; Deephouse & Jaskiewicz, 2013). The papers that integrate organization theories represent the only qualitative papers in the set (four), whereas we found again mostly quantitative studies (eighteen) and only one conceptual paper.

3.2.3 Challenger

The *Challenger* type of FB papers targets a management scholar audience in theoretical domains other than family business. The main goal of this type of paper is to show how the distinctive nature of family firms can alter, extend, and/ or modify the well-established predictions and assumptions of existing theories. Papers belonging to this type of research explain phenomena well known in the general management literature audience, but whose peculiarities and dynamics in the family business context have not yet been established. In other words, scholars who write this type of FB research *challenge* general management knowledge and try to understand how the distinctive characteristics of family firms affect the theoretical phenomena of interest.

This relatively small set of papers has been highly influential in establishing the FB field as a rigorous and theoretically driven field of academic research. Pivotal early FB researchers, such as Luis Gómez-Mejia, Pascual Berrone, and James Chrisman, introduced the idea that family ownership matters because of the SEW attached to family ownership, which influences all kinds of strategic decisions. Those researchers questioned some of the assumptions and predictions of existing corporate governance and strategic management theories in the context of family firms and contributed to establishing family ownership as an important boundary condition (e.g., Carney & Gedajlovic, 2002; Chrisman et al., 2012; Gomez-Mejia et al., 2001, 2007; Strike et al., 2015). In this set of studies, we find seminal papers such as the study of 2001, where Gomez-Mejia et al. presented to management audience a variant of the agency contract that involves family ties between the principal and the agent, or Gomez-Mejia et al. (2007), where they challenged general management literature by claiming that family ownership matters and introduced the concept of SEW. The paper by Gomez-Mejia et al. (2007) challenged extant formulations of the behavioral agency model and advanced the understanding of agency problems in family firms.

Follow-up papers have provided further opportunities for theoretical refinement by applying these arguments to a wide array of strategic decisions and behaviors. For instance, Berrone et al. (2010) explained differences in CSR in family firms and Chrisman and Patel (2012) explained variations in R&D investments of family and nonfamily firms. Similarly, Strike et al. (2015) identified boundary conditions to agency theory by highlighting the importance idiosyncratic characteristics of owners and managers (i.e., their affiliation to the family owning the firm) as factors that affect CEOs' strategic decisions and career. Along the same lines, Chirico et al. (2020) examined business exit choices and refined further behavioral agency theory by considering the affective motives of family owners.

Other researchers have shown the validity of SEW arguments and the influence of family involvement in the business in several other settings. For instance, Jaskiewicz et al. (2017a) extends knowledge on Top Management Team pay dispersion and firm performance by looking at the influence of family ownership. Along the same lines, Anderson and Reeb (2004) consider the role of the family nature of the firm in determining the performance implications of the composition of the board of directors, advancing general management knowledge on the determinants of firm performance.

Where Is Organization Theory? The Challenger set of papers continue to show a surprising lack of OT frameworks. We could not find articles that challenge or refine classical organization theories. Most often, FB scholars draw on those frameworks (e.g., institutional theory) to explain firm heterogeneity or institutional pressures. This conversation may be occurring in specialized journals, but to our knowledge it has not yet reached the readers of generalist management outlets.

3.2.4 Generalized

The fourth type of paper is one where the "family firm" represents an (often ideal) empirical setting to examine theoretical research questions of interest for management scholars. In this type of paper, there are insights to be gained for family business scholars, but the main goal is to examine this setting as an exemplar case of a broader phenomenon.

Papers presenting *generalized* research contribute to extending knowledge in a nonfamily theoretical domain (i.e., advancing theory that does not specifically pertain to family business) (e.g., Cruz et al., 2010; Luo et al., 2019). The family business is a setting to isolate the phenomenon and study it (e.g., Chung & Luo, 2008; Eddleston et al., 2020; Patel & Cooper, 2014; Petriglieri & Stein, 2012).

For example, the papers by Cruz et al. (2010) and Luo et al. (2019) advance agency theory. The former does so by integrating a trust perspective within agency theory to study contracts at the TMT level (Cruz et al., 2010). The latter draws on an institutional logics perspective and provides boundary conditions to agency theory with respect to analysts' coverage decisions about family-controlled firms (Luo et al., 2019). According to the authors, the predictions based on agency theory hold only when the analyst firms' home-country institutional logics of corporate governance is consistent with the agency theory assumptions. Both papers test their hypotheses in a family business setting, and this choice is justified by the opportunity granted by this context to produce better proxies for theoretical constructs (e.g., TMT uncertainty and higher risk of coverage by analysts).

Many other studies in this group focus on phenomena not specifically unique to family firms but for which family business represents suitable contexts for examination. This is, for instance, the case of the study of equality in structural power in upper echelons (Patel & Cooper, 2014). Family businesses are indeed ideal to study the distribution of structural power among TMT members due to the typical presence of both family and nonfamily managers. Patel and Cooper (2014) investigate a topic of interest for any type of firm (i.e., equality in structural power) but build on a dimension of diversity that exists only in family firms (i.e., the affiliation of the managers to the family owning the firm). In so doing, while focusing on a peculiar characteristic of family firms, the authors contribute to general management literature, yielding results that are generalizable to any other individual characteristic giving rise to diversity. Other examples of this type of study are the works by Eddleston et al. (2020), who draw upon sensemaking theory to study the engagement in payment of briberies by entrepreneurs, and Petriglieri and Stein (2012), who analyze the case of the Gucci family business and study the development and maintenance of a leader's identity through a psychodynamic perspective.

Although the positioning and contribution of *generalist* papers is to the general management literature, contributions to the family business literature may also be highlighted. Arregle et al. (2007) contribute to the analysis of family firms' uniqueness by investigating the mechanisms that link a family's social capital to the creation of social capital in the family firm and the factors underlying this creation. Li and Piezunka (2020) contribute to research on family business by clarifying which network structure may be most conducive to positive synergies between family and firm in intergenerational leadership succession. These examples address research questions of interest for management scholars, while also providing ancillary contributions to the family business field.

Where Is Organization Theory? This final group of papers provides more examples of an eclectic use of OT frameworks. Theories that scholars have advanced by examining family business settings include sensemaking to study corruption (Eddleston et al., 2020), networks (Li & Piezunka, 2020), institutional logics (Chung & Luo, 2008; Luo et al., 2019), leaders' identity work (Petriglieri & Stein, 2012), organizational power and control (Ainsworth & Cox, 2003), gender (Byrne et al., 2021), and moral legitimacy (Richards et al., 2017). In comparison to other groups, we found more qualitative papers (six): nine papers were quantitative, and two conceptual.

3.3 Renewing the Call for Coupling

Overall, this section has helped reveal that OT is not particularly well represented in the FB literature published in top management generalist journals. Scholars who belong to the FB community and explore phenomena of interest for family firms (e.g., the specific and evergreen issue of succession) have not leveraged classical theories of organizations or its more recent developments in a substantial way. Theoretical preference has been given to strategic and behavioral frameworks. OT scholars, on the other hand, have only occasionally considered family enterprises as settings where OT frameworks could be applied or explored opportunities for integration between OT and FB theories. In this final section, we rekindle the call for coupling between OT and FB. We do so by reviewing and expanding the suggestions offered by Salvato et al. in the 2019 Special Issue of *Organization Studies*. We categorize these suggestions into our 2×2 matrix, to reveal the wide array of contributions they can provide (Table 5). In the final section of this Element, we will zoom in into potential areas of overlap between the two fields.

Salvato et al. (2019) identified five key features of family businesses that offer promising areas of potential cross-fertilization – family ownership, family governance and management, transgenerational intent, generational involvement, and perceived family identity. Each of these elements offer opportunities for a deeper examination of family business dynamics (for FB scholars) or an extension/revision of existing theories (for OT scholars). Interestingly, each quadrant reveals a unique modality of augmenting theory and advance knowledge.

Embedded – Introducing New Concepts. In the case of an embedded type of contribution, FB scholars can address important phenomena that concern FB by extending the array of theoretical concepts they draw on. For example, Salvato et al. (2019) provide examples of organizational concepts that can expand the theoretical breadth of FB research in strategic decisions such as downsizing or divestiture. These concepts may have been overlooked or neglected when other dominant paradigms are used. Along the same lines, research on succession (e.g., transgenerational intent, generational involvement) can be examined with a fresh look by introducing concepts related to goal multiplicity and legitimacy. OT offers a wide array of theoretical concepts that can be very useful when applied to FB research questions.

Integrative – Introducing New Theories. In the case of an integrative type of contribution, both OT and FB scholars can learn from each other. Salvato et al. (2019)'s suggestions point to the use of theoretical frameworks that are not typically part of the FB repertoire, but that can shed new light on important questions about FB strategies and behaviors. Organizational identity (OI), for instance, is a theoretical framework that can yield numerous insights and is being increasingly drawn upon by FB scholars. Other theories (e.g., resource partitioning from population ecology) are rarely used and can be leveraged more extensively. For instance, this scholarly community has been very influential in shaping research on categorization, which fits very well research on authenticity and craft industries in FB.

Challenger – Introducing New Boundary Conditions. For a challenger type of contribution, the dialogue between OT and FB scholars is particularly useful to identify boundary conditions to extant theories. Thus far, most of these contributions have refined theories of corporate governance and the behavioral agency model (CEO duality, R&D investment, business exit). Understanding how family ownership and involvement in management may alter existing theoretical predictions is still very much an open task. Some organization theories have begun to be assessed by including the family variable (e.g., responses to institutional pressures for CSR in family and nonfamily businesses). Many others have not.

Generalized – Introducing New Settings. Finally, organization studies can really benefit from examining FB settings in a generalized contribution. Family business settings provide some unique characteristics that may help scholars unpack broader organizational phenomena. For instance, issues of identity and identification are particularly salient in FB, as are multiplex relationships. Theories of tradition, institutional guardianship (Dacin et al., 2019), industry persistence and revival (Raffaelli, 2019) can find ideal settings in industries with a prevalence of family enterprises or FB organizations, as can theories of strategic narratives (Vaara et al., 2016) and craft (Kroezen et al., 2021). Theories of paradox and strategic renewal are also particularly fitting for FB settings (Raffaelli et al., 2021).

4 Suggestions for Advancing FB Research through Organization Theories and Advancing OT through Family Business Research

As highlighted in Section 2, the family business literature has examined many key issues related to family business firms. The purpose of this Element is to push the conversation beyond the boundaries of the family business field. Our aim is to offer useful and constructive ideas for scholars on both sides of the aisle to engage in multiple conversations around the four types of contributions we discussed in Section 3: embedded, integrative, challenger, and generalized.

In Section 4, we examine three theoretical domains that we see as particularly fruitful to develop engaging conversations between the two fields: (i) hybridity; (ii) tensions, dualities, and paradoxes; and (iii) time and temporality. These domains have enriched the OT literature (or are rapidly gaining traction) and, we believe, resonate particularly well with the core areas of concerns and attention of FB scholars. Specifically, *hybridity* speaks directly to the need in family enterprises to manage the presence of two complex systems, that is, the family and the business systems. *Tensions, dualities*, and *paradoxes* are core to the strategic challenge in family firms to manage elements that are in apparent

Table 5 Opportunities for coupling between OT and FB

	CONTRIBUTION TO?	
CONTEXTUAL ORIENTATION? Context-specific	**FB audience**	**MGMT audience**
	EMBEDDED Family Ownership ✓ Include a *socio-cognitive perspective* to research on FB downsizing Family Management/Governance ✓ Include *organizational concepts (threat-rigidity hypotheses; escalation of commitment)* into research on FB divestiture Transgenerational Intent ✓ Include a *temporal orientation perspective* into research on FB succession Generational Involvement ✓ Include concepts of *goal multiplicity and goal alignment* into studies of generational involvement ✓ Include *rhetoric and narrative* in negotiating relationship between generations Perceived FB identity ✓ Include concepts of *organizational legitimacy* into examinations of the FB identity	**CHALLENGER** Family Ownership ✓ Examine how family ownership affect theories of downsizing ✓ Examine how family ownership moderates *resource partitioning theory* Family Management/Governance ✓ Consider how family management affects predictions of *CEO duality* ✓ Consider how family management affects *divestitures decisions*

INTEGRATIVE

Family Ownership

✓ Integrate *theories of professional archetypes* to examine how ownership affects professionalization in FB

✓ Integrate *resource partitioning theory* to explain how family heritage and culture sustain FB amidst industry dynamics

Transgenerational Intent

✓ Integrate *theories of identity paradoxes* to understand negotiation of conflicting identities

Perceived FB identity

✓ Integrate *theories of identity work* to understand internal and external perceptions of FB

✓ Integrate *theories of identity and reputation* into research on FB heterogeneity and difference with non-FB

GENERALIZED

Family Ownership

✓ Qualify extant *theories of professional archetypes* by studying FB settings

Transgenerational Intent

✓ Extend research on *temporal work* by examining FB settings

Perceived FB identity

✓ Extend research on *identity work* by examining FB settings

Theory specific

Revision by the Authors from Salvato et al. (2019)

trade-offs or competition with one another (e.g., financial, and nonfinancial goals, innovation, and tradition). *Time* and *temporality* are central issues to the pursuit of continuity and longevity in firms that simultaneously look back and forward. These theoretical challenges can be better understood by drawing on insights from the FB literature and family firms as settings; in turn, FB research can be significantly advanced by drawing and integrating insights from these streams of OT work. We discuss opportunities for cross-fertilization in those three areas: (i) *managing hybridity*; (ii) *mastering tensions, dualities, and paradoxes*; and (iii) *modeling time and temporality.*

4.1 Managing Hybridity

In the OT literature, hybrid organizations have gained much interest because the combination of seemingly incompatible elements presents an interesting puzzle for organizational scholars. For a detailed examination of the literature on hybrids, we recommend the comprehensive reviews by Battilana and Lee (2014) and Battilana et al. (2017). These reviews identify three main theoretical perspectives that have been used to address hybridity: hybrids as the combination of *institutional logics* (Battilana & Dorado, 2010; Greenwood et al., 2011; Pache & Santos, 2013), *identities* (Albert & Whetten, 1985; Glynn, 2000; Whetten et al., 2014), and *organizational forms* (Ruef & Patterson, 2009; Tracey & Phillips, 2011).

In the first perspective, hybridity is the combination of broader societal-level rationales, that is, institutional logics, that define values and behavioral prescriptions for individuals and organizations. This approach looks at the extra-organizational level of analysis as a source of hybridity and the impact of such multiplicity at the organizational level. The second perspective focuses on hybridity in identities, mostly at the intraorganizational level, and treats hybridity as multiple shared views about "who we are." Finally, the organizational form perspective refers to hybrids as " . . . organizational arrangements that use resources and/or governance structures from more than one existing organization" (Borys & Jemison, 1989, p. 235). In this perspective, hybridity is considered either a combination of distinct forms or governance, ownership, and control, or, in a more interpretive understanding, the combination of elements from two or more socially constructed categories or archetypes.

Several of these concepts are applicable to family business firms. It is relatively surprising that not much effort has been made in this direction, with some notable exceptions. Since its inception, scholars in the family business field have agreed that the core feature of family businesses is the combination of two subsystems of family and business. This feature significantly influences the behaviors of these organizations (Leaptrott, 2005; Pieper & Klein, 2007; Sharma, 2004; Tagiuri & Davis, 1996). A family's involvement as owners, managers, and employees in the business is a key factor that uniquely distinguishes them from nonfamily businesses (Astrachan et al., 2002; Chua et al., 1999; Shanker & Astrachan, 1996). Whereas this element of complexity has been at the forefront of family business research for a long time, scholars have looked only relatively recently at family firms as "hybrid organizations" and tried to understand the unique challenges and opportunities that come from hybridity. From an organizational lens, the focus is not on determining how family involvement may shape behaviors and strategies of family firms. The focus is on how these organizations *manage hybridity.* We review the three perspectives that have been used to conceptualize hybridity in OT and discuss them vis-à-vis the family business literature. We discuss the nature of the hybridity of family businesses and draw on the literature on hybrid organizing to discuss how family firms can manage hybridity. In fact, what is a hybrid and what makes a family firm a hybrid need to be specified before we can move forward. The focus on this section is therefore the following:

Research Focus: (a) *How does research in family business inform knowledge on hybrids and hybridization in OT?* (b) *How does OT research on hybrids advance knowledge on the way family businesses manage the hybridity stemming from the combination of the family and business systems?*

4.1.1 Hybrid as Combination of Logics

The first perspective – hybrid as combination of institutional logics – is rooted in the institutional literature. From the vantage point of institutionalists, organizations are embedded in a broader environment that provides both constraints and opportunities to them. Specifically, institutional logics are overarching sets of principles that prescribe "how to interpret organizational reality, what constitutes appropriate behavior, and how to succeed" (Thornton, 2004, p. 70); see also Friedland and Alford (1991). Logics provide guidelines on how to interpret and function in social situations. Organizations comply with logics to gain endorsement from important referent audiences and because logics provide a lens to understand the social world and act confidently. The institutional literature emphasizes the multiplicity of logics in the environment and discusses how organizations face multiple logics that may – or may not – be mutually incompatible (Friedland & Alford, 1991; Kraatz & Block, 2008). When organizations confront prescriptions from multiple institutional logics that are deemed incompatible, they face institutional complexity (Greenwood et al., 2011).

Institutional complexity generates challenges and tensions for organizations exposed to them. For example, organizations like community banks or social enterprises are embedded in multiple logics that have important implications for their strategies and behaviors. Community banks are embedded in two highly influential logics: the financial or economic logic (Thornton & Ocasio, 1999) and the local or community-based logic (Marquis & Lounsbury, 2007). There are evident challenges and opportunities associated with hybridity. Almandoz (2012), for instance, showed the benefits and problems associated with embeddedness of founding teams of banks in both logics during peaceful and turbulent times. He found that in economically stable periods, founding teams highly embedded in both logics are more likely to establish their bank. By contrast, in economically turbulent periods, founding teams highly embedded in both logics are more likely to withdraw. Similarly, social enterprises are hybrid organizations that pursue the dual mission of achieving both financial sustainability and social purpose, thus facing the conflicting prescriptions of commercial and social logics (Battilana & Dorado, 2010; Doherty et al., 2014). Studies show that embeddedness in both logics creates challenges in terms of possibility of mission drift but can also ensure flexibility in terms of resource acquisition, by providing multiple sources and a stream of highly motivated volunteers.

Most of the literature on hybrids from an institutional perspective has focused on the *strategies* that organizations use to manage the incompatibility of competing external demands. These include compromising, avoiding, defying, and manipulating (Jay, 2013; Pache & Santos, 2013), and deleting, compartmentalizing, aggregating, and synthesizing to cope with internal identity struggles (Jay, 2013; Kraatz & Block, 2008). Interestingly, recent studies such as Cappellaro et al. (2020) have pointed at longitudinal *processes of hybridization*. Their study of an Italian hospital is built on the observation that organizations are not always born hybrids and they may not be effectively integrated, as prior work suggests. In their ethnographic study, they shed light on the temporal unfolding of hybridization and/or de-hybridization and highlight the powerful role of feedback – both positive and negative – from external audiences.

Logics in the Family Business Literature. Turning to the family business literature, the logics perspective has been applied to family businesses, but in a selective way and by only a handful of authors. Critically, not much has been written about hybridity as combination of logics. Back in 2011, Greenwood et al. (2011) were among the first scholars to foreshadow the idea of institutional complexity and to note how nonmarket institutions and logics have been particularly missing from the management literature. As the authors argued, "we know relatively little about the influence of institutions such as the *family*, religion, and the state on contemporary organizations" (2011, p. 521). The institutional logic of the family is defined by Friedland and Alford (1991, p. 248) as "a set of cultural rules and assumptions associated with notions of community and unconditional loyalty to family members and their reproductive needs." This familial logic has been characterized as one of "nurturing, generativity, and loyalty to the family" (Miller et al., 2011, p. 4).

Greenwood et al. (2011)'s study was pivotal in showing that logics are historically contingent and that understanding context-specific logics is essential to explain organizational responses to market logics. Specifically, their explanation of downsizing practices in Spanish firms would have been truncated without considering the Catholic tradition and its emphasis on paternalistic family values. At the time of the study, the idea that family-managed firms behave differently toward their workforces was not fully established. Their hypotheses about the influence of family management on organizational practices were fully supported and revealed two main insights. First, the strength of the institution of the family in Spain influences organizational decisions about downsizing. Specifically, family-managed firms are less likely to downsize than nonfamily-managed firms. Second, professionalization of family firms may lead them to support practices that in principle would be at odds with the social norms of family firms. In fact, the authors found that the tendency for family-managed firms not to downsize is less pronounced in large firms. Contrary to the authors' expectations, the interaction between family logics and regional pressures was not significant, suggesting that the effects of the two nonmarket institutional logics may be independent of each other.

Following this study, other authors have highlighted the paucity of research on family logics in organization studies. Fairclough and Micelotta (2013), for example, noted that institutional researchers have rarely examined the institutional logics of the family and they "have followed in the footsteps of family business research by implicitly reinforcing the notion that familial logic is integral to these firms' practices and that it shapes only family firms' behaviors and strategic choices." (2013, p. 382). Notably, there has been very little attempt to examine the impact of the institutional logic of the family on nonfamily firms, even though they are embedded in societal family logics as well.

In the family business domain, a few studies have drawn upon the notion of institutional logic (Jaskiewicz et al., 2016; Reay et al., 2015; Zellweger et al., 2016). Reay et al. (2015) examined the multiplicity of institutional logics in which wineries in British Columbia are embedded. They examined how family, business, and community logics interact in influencing family firm behavior. Specifically, they found that different firms were guided by different arrangements of logics. Traditional family firms drew moderately strongly on all three logics; lifestyle family firms drew strongly on the family logic, only moderately on the business logic and weakly on the community logic; non-family firms drew strongly on the business logic and weakly on the community logic, but not on the family logic. The authors also reveal the actions taken by these companies to maintain legitimacy and sustainability over time. Along the same lines, Jaskiewicz et al. (2016) used the notion of logics to study succession and argue that conflicts between family and commercial logics lead to different succession processes. The study identifies four approaches that family firms use to manage coexisting family and commercial logics as succession becomes imminent: the interwoven approach, the selective approach, the commercial approach, and the detached approach. Different succession outcomes are associated with each approach, in terms of successful transfer of the business or sale of the business and end of family ownership. A micro foundation approach to logics is also adopted by Zellweger et al. (2016) to explore the multidimensionality of the family logic in pricing decisions during intergenerational successions. The authors argue for a more nuanced understanding of the family logic, beyond a monolithic view of norms of parental altruism, loyalty, and paternalism. Specifically, they draw on the work of family sociologists such as Bengtson and Achenbaum (1993) and Kohli and Künemund (2003) to suggest four central family norms: parental altruism, parents' self-interested expectations for the future, filial reciprocity, and filial duty (filial piety). In their view, family norms entail contradictory indications of what constitutes a legitimate family discount, and this element represents an important, but under-investigated, form of institutional complexity. Finally, Miller et al. (2017, 2011) compared the logics of family members and lone founders and use them as "social context" to understand their impact on growth strategies of these firms.

Research Opportunities. Although robust and insightful, these studies hint at hybridity, but do not frame family businesses as hybrid organizations. This is a key point recently made by Boers and Nordqvist (2012), who pointed out how using some of the frameworks and insights of the hybridity literature may be incredibly useful to shed light on the nature, extent, and underlying dynamics of heterogeneity in family firms. As an illustration, they draw on the framework developed by Besharov and Smith (2014) and the classification of hybrid into four different types based on the degree of logic compatibility and logic centrality: contested, estranged, aligned, and dominant organizations. This is one example of how the theoretical tools provided by the hybridity literature allow researchers to develop new insights. The logics and hybridity frameworks can be used to develop different contributions. For instance:

- **RQs for Embedded Studies:**
  - *How do configurations of hybridity map into existing studies of heterogeneity in family firms?* *Existing dimensions of hybridity can be mapped into the dimensions of logics.
  - *How do family firms combine different logics? What hybridity strategies do they use? Are hybridity strategies different from nonfamily firms?*
  - *How does the management of hybridity affect outcomes (e.g., innovation, performance, longevity)?* *The literature on hybridity can shed light on drivers and sources of heterogeneity and reveal unique managing strategies in family firms.
- **RQs for Integrative Studies:**
  - *How do family firms develop a dynamic capability to manage hybridity?* *Integrating a dynamic capability perspective can help us understand hybridity in family firms as a capability that organizations develop.
  - *How does resource orchestration enable family firms to navigate hybridity (over their lifecycle)?* *Integrating a resource perspective can shed light on the role of resources in managing hybridity; the additional lifecycle perspective can shed light on this process from a longitudinal perspective.
- **RQs for Challenger Studies:**
  - *How does family involvement change theories of "mission drift" in hybrid organizations?* *Family enterprises are durable hybrids, seemingly less susceptible to mission drift compared to, for instance, social enterprises.
  - *How do family firms (as hybrid organizations spanning categories) extend/refine/challenge categorization theory?* *Family firms may show different *processes* and outcomes of categorization, thus extending knowledge on mechanisms of categorization.
- **RQs for Generalized Studies:**
  - *How does a diverse array of actors actively maintain coherence and durability of logics in a hybrid organization?* *Family enterprise is an ideal setting to examine a durable hybrid organization and extend the logics literature in hybrid organizations.

4.1.2 Hybrid as Combination of Identities

The second perspective considers hybridity as the combination of distinctly different identity categories. As explained by Whetten et al. (2014, p. 480), hybrid-identity organizations (HIOs) "challenge the 'coherence premise' of identity theory – i.e., that an actor's identity provides a strong foundation upon which a coherent (temporally and spatially consistent) set of beliefs, attitudes, and actions can be built." OI represents members' self-definitions of their organization, and it provides a consensual answer to the question "who are we?." OI is also generally recognized by other audiences, who see who the organization is and what it is about (Gioia et al., 2010; Whetten, 2006). Identity has been characterized by three distinct attributes of being central, enduring, and distinct. Central means that identity encapsulates what core and essential about an organization, not peripheral elements. Enduring means that identity reflects core elements that have a persistent nature, rather than being ephemeral and transitory. Distinct means that identity consists of a set of features that characterize what makes the organization what it is and explain what makes it similar to, and different from, others.

The notion of hybridity complicates this picture substantially. HIOs equally embody two distinct social forms and their members consider themselves as being both a Type A and a Type B organization. Examples include symphony orchestras (Glynn, 2000), social enterprises (Moss et al., 2011), and microfinance development associations (Battilana & Dorado, 2010). One of the discussion points in the literature has been what distinguishes hybrids from other organizations that may display multiple identities. Notably, Albert et al. (Albert, 1998; Albert & Adams, 2002) suggested that, compared to other organizations, HIOs possess the "3Is." The first feature is the degree to which two or more of their identities are generally considered to be *incompatible*. Some organizations may have dual identities, but if those are highly related identities (such as a church relief agency), the organization cannot be considered a HIO. For hybrids, the identities should be considered at least incongruous and inconsistent, if not utterly incompatible. The second feature is the *indispensable* role of each identity, which makes it impossible to eliminate or delete either one when conflict arises between the two. The final feature is that hybrid identities are *inviolate*, in the sense that they conform to social expectations that provide prescriptions and proscriptions on how that kind of organization is supposed to behave (King & Whetten, 2008). HIOs are particularly challenged because they may pay a very high social discount for not conforming to societal expectations that are associated with *both* their identities. HIOs must work out internal arrangements that make these elements coherent internally, while simultaneously conforming to the expectations of a diverse set of stakeholders to maintain legitimacy.

Similar to how Besharov and Smith (2014) classified hybrids based on the degree of logic compatibility and logic centrality, Albert et al.' work sheds light on the heterogeneity in the population of HIOs. These authors focus on two attributes: the degree to which incompatible identities are structurally integrated, and the extent to which decision makers establish priorities for resolving identity conflicts. The first dimension (also referred to as "Locus of Duality") identifies hybrid organizations as either "ideographic" or "holographic." Ideographic identities are segregated (A+B) and distinct subgroups and/or separate units hold each identity. "Holographic" organizations are integrated (A×B) and all members and units hold multiple identities, rather than just one. The second dimension – the degree of identity priority (also referred to as "Order of Duality") – focuses on the importance assigned to the HIO's multiple identities. In other words, if the organization has established a priori ordering of their identity claims, there is the presence of "trumping rights" indicated as "High: Ab/aB." In this scenario, identities are unequal. Conversely, if there is no a priori ordering of identities, the organization has not established trumping rights and the scenario is identifies as "Low: AB." The classification of hybrid organizations reveals how different types of hybrids prioritize competing identity claims and manage conflicts between these identities.

In their literature review of hybrid organizations, Battilana et al. found that most of the empirical research from this perspective focuses on the ideographic type and emphasizes hybrid identities as sources of conflict and contestation between distinct subgroups (e.g., Anteby & Wrzesniewski, 2014; Ashforth & Reingen, 2014; Pratt & Rafaeli, 1997).

Identity(ies) in the Family Business Literature. Turning to the family business literature, the investigation of identity in this domain is still in its infancy (e.g., Abdelgawad & Zahra, 2020; Dieleman & Koning, 2019; Prügl & Spitzley, 2021; Sasaki et al., 2020). Early on, the concept of OI was introduced as a complementing dimension of familiness (Zellweger et al., 2010). The integration of the family and business identities is considered a unique and differentiating feature of family firms, although not always a positive one. These two identities can provide benefits such as strong organizational culture and unique values (Sundaramurthy & Kreiner, 2008), or generate conflicts that harm the organization (Habbershon & Williams, 1999; Sundaramurthy & Kreiner, 2008).

More recently, scholars have begun to consider family businesses as embodying multiple identities (Shepherd & Haynie, 2009; Sundaramurthy & Kreiner, 2008). Shepherd and Haynie (2009) theorized a family-business meta-identity that reconciles "who we are as a family" with "who we are as a business," thus defining "who we are as a family business." Notably, some authors have explicitly used family businesses to exemplify HIOs (Boers & Nordqvist, 2012; Dyer Jr. & Whetten, 2006). Most of this work has been conceptual, however. Whetten et al. (2014), for instance, identify family firms as HIOs that combine identity elements of the "family" and "business" social forms or categories. Their insights are highly relevant for family business scholarship as they suggest using the OI framework and their classification of HIOs to better understand heterogeneity of family firms and how identity-related conflicts can be addressed. Boers and Nordqvist (2012) reiterate the usefulness of the notion of hybrid identities to explore the heterogeneity of the population of family firms (Melin & Nordqvist, 2007; Sharma & Nordqvist, 2007). Specifically, they suggest that family-controlled firms listed on the stock market behave differently. This is due to their hybrid identity, which influences the self-understanding of the business and steers their governance. The illustrative case discussed by the authors reveals how a hybrid character develops over time, as the company transitioned from being a family firm controlled by a family, to a private equity firm.

Finally, there is also an emerging interest in understanding heterogeneity and dynamic processes of hybridity in family firms in response to disruptive innovations. The conceptual paper by Brinkerink et al. (2020) categorizes family firms archetypically as either family businesses – in which OI is largely defined by the operational activities performed – or business families, where the operational activities are less central to the family firm's OI – (cf. Le Breton-Miller & Miller, 2018). They build on this distinction to theorize the construct of "organizational identity elasticity," which reflects the degree to which two fundamental elements of OI are coupled: "who we are" and "what we do." The two archetypes are classified at the extreme of the OI elasticity. Family firms whose dominant coalition holds a very inelastic OI perception will construe their sense of self in terms of the family firm's core activities (i.e., family businesses). Conversely, family firms with a more elastic OI will focus on pursuing wealth for the family and sustainability across generations. The company's core activities play a much more instrumental role in catering to other more identity-defining features of the organization, thus reinforcing the association with the business family archetype. An interesting contribution of this Element is that it presents OI as a multifaceted and dynamic concept. The Element reveals how a family business differs from a business family in framing and responding to change, but also how a family business may develop into a business family, and vice versa, as a consequence of its strategic decisions and OI work (e.g., Dieleman & Koning, 2019).

Research Opportunities. There are multiple opportunities to extend research on family firms as an archetypal form of organization characterized by multiple identities (HIOs). For instance:

- **RQs for Embedded Studies:**
  - *How do family firms prioritize competing identity claims and manage conflicts between these identities?* *A key question for family enterprises is how multiple identities can be managed and prioritized.

○ *How do milestone events in a family firm (e.g., succession, M&A, IPOs, sale of the business, changes in the family) affect hybrid identities? How does identity work enable family firms to respond to threats to their identities?* *Episodes that trigger organizational change reveal identity dynamics in family enterprises.

- **RQs for Integrative Studies:**
  ○ *What is the role of imprinting in maintaining identity hybridity in family firms?* *Integrating an imprinting perspective can shed light on the effect of founders and early environmental events on hybridity.
  ○ *How does identity work and boundary work enable family firms to manage identity hybridity?* *Integrating both the perspective of identity and boundary work can shed light on when and how identities can be compartmentalized or assimilated.

- **RQs for Challenger Studies:**
  ○ *How does family involvement extend theories of identity formation and change?* *Family enterprises are HIOs and can extend current theories of identity.
  ○ *How do family firms (as typically holographic hybrid organizations with integrated multiple identities) extend/refine/challenge HIO theory?* *Family firms are archetypal of organizations where the two identities are rarely segregated.

- **RQs for Generalized Studies:**
  ○ *How is a HIO constructed?* *Family firms are an ideal setting to examine the construction of an organization that is born as a hybrid.
  ○ *How does a HIO strategically leverage hybrid identities to survive a scandal that threatens its existence?* *Family firms offer ideal settings to examine identity and image dynamics under duress.

4.1.3 Hybrid as Combination of Organizational Forms

The third perspective considers hybridity as the combination of established organizational forms. This line of research has drawn from different theoretical perspectives, but the common thread is that the locus of analysis of hybridity is the organization's structures and practices. For example, scholars in the TCE tradition have looked at hybrids as an intermediate form of economic organization combining market and hierarchical forms of governance, for example, franchise (Shane, 1996; Williamson, 1985). Network scholars have described hybridity as the combination of network and hierarchy (Adler, 2001; Podolny & Page, 1998), and looked at the mixing of governance, ownership, and control through network forms, as in alliances and other interorganizational relationships (Gereffi et al., 2005).

Organizational theorists have looked at hybrids in three different ways, highlighting the structural aspect, the category aspect, and the archetype aspect. Greenwood et al. (2011) revisited the ambidexterity literature and structural-contingency arguments and saw potential in the distinction between two types of structures – "blended" and "structurally differentiated" hybrids, with the former combining and layering "practices" and the latter partitioning/compartmentalizing them into the subunits of an organization (see also Simsek, 2009). A second line of work draws on population ecology and the category literature to define hybrids as forms that combine features associated with multiple social categories of organizational forms (Hannan et al., 2007; Minkoff, 2002; Ruef, 2000; Ruef & Patterson, 2009). For example, biotechnology companies combine features of academic research organizations and business organizations (Murray, 2010; Powell & Sandholtz, 2012), or nanotechnology start-ups integrate features of two distinct categories: science and technology (Wry et al., 2014). Finally, the organizational archetypes perspective looks at hybrids as organizations that combine archetypal configurations of organizational structures and practices that are internally consistent and coherent with the institutional context (Greenwood et al., 1993; Greenwood & Suddaby, 2006; Tolbert et al., 2011). Interestingly, this perspective has been often drawn upon in the growing empirical literature on social enterprises that blend for-profit and nonprofit archetypes (Mair et al., 2012; Tracey & Phillips, 2011), and to provide a fresh perspective on State-Owned Enterprises (SOEs) who consist of different mixtures of private ownership and control by the state (Bruton et al., 2015; Huang & Orr, 2007).

Organizational Forms in the Family Business Literature. Turning to the family business literature, the classical approach has been to explain the nexus between family business and business family in terms of archetypal organizational forms (e.g., Le Breton-Miller & Miller, 2018). Researchers consider that many of the unique challenges facing family-owned firms flow from the overlap between these systems. Hence the importance of the boundaries between the systems, which are critical to regulate that overlap (e.g., Bork et al., 1996). Early research in this domain depicted family and business as a duality and suggested the need to manage this dichotomy by strategically prioritizing one or the other: either family first or business first (Ward, 1997). Dunn (1995) also subscribed to this position and interpreted the family–business relationship as a theoretical continuum. At one extreme, the family philosophy dominates, and management and governance decisions are subordinated. At the other end, the business philosophy dominates. As a result, there has been a strong effort in the literature to distinguish family enterprises from nonfamily enterprises, and from one another by classifying family firms and clarify the nature of their governance and business systems. Typologies show how family relationships influence the way an organization is structured, governed, and managed (Hoffman et al., 2006). The key effort has been to understand how the business is affected by integration, overlap, or resource sharing with the family system (e.g., Bizri, 2016; Habbershon & Williams, 1999; Powell & Eddleston, 2017).

Since then, scholars have shifted mindset and there is now a more shared understanding that the family and business systems need simultaneous attention (Dyer Jr. & Whetten, 2006) and should be viewed as inextricably entwined (Aldrich & Cliff, 2003). Zody et al. (2006) offered an interesting discussion of the role of boundaries, highlighting that there are competing arguments about whether rigid boundaries are needed in order to avoid the possibility that family problems will affect business performance (Weigel & Ballard-Reisch, 1997). Other scholars argue for more integration between family and business systems. Basco and Pérez Rodríguez (2009) theorized and empirically confirmed that emphasis on both family and business systems in four areas of management and governance – strategy, board governance, human resources, and succession – leads to better performance. However, there are still very few empirical examinations of boundaries. Thus far, the most typical approach to managing the hybridity of family firms as combining family and business systems has been focused on corporate governance and control (see Aguilera & Crespi-Cladera, 2012). This research draws from agency theory, which stipulates that ownership (e.g., family, state, investors, banks) is associated with different interests. Critically, family owners have a strong interest in keeping ownership and control of the firm. As many studies have shown, family ownership has a profound effect on governance practices: family-managed firms deploy fewer formal monitoring and control mechanisms; they rely less on external auditors to monitor managerial decisions and particular importance is given to the to board of directors, whose functioning and tasks significantly affect the direction that firms take (e.g., Arzubiaga et al., 2018).

In a recent comprehensive book on management of family firms for a wide audience of practitioners and academics, Zellweger asserts that family firms need an "integrated governance system" (2017, p. 106) that weaves the domains of corporate, ownership, family, and wealth governance into a coherent framework (see also Jaskiewicz & Rau, 2021). Importantly, this Element highlights that governance systems are different at different stages in the lifetime of family firms. As family firms go through the stages of owner-manager, sibling partnership, cousin consortium, and family enterprise, the challenges associated with corporate and family governance differ. In terms of managing hybridity, a key insight we can take from this Element is that both the family and the business systems require their own governance structure and process. The business system needs structures in place such as the board of directors to ensure the efficient cooperation of board members, managers, and shareholders. The family system needs structures such as family councils and family assemblies to ensure the efficient cooperation of family members and the management of family involvement in management and ownership. The integration of family and business systems is critical to ensure a smooth running and prevents many of the conflicting relationships that unfortunately still plague family firms.

It is relevant to mention that the importance of managing effectively family systems, rather than considering them as ancillary to the business system, is partially due to the renewed push from some scholars to pay closer attention to the "family." To this end, researchers point to interdisciplinary research known as family science, which focuses on familial relationships (e.g., cohesion, communication, conflict), family member roles (e.g., parents, children, siblings), family transitions (e.g., marriage, divorce, birth of a child, retirement), and important outcomes for families (e.g., children's health and academic performance, marital health). Notably, these scholars suggest that family science theories might help explain how differences in families shape differences among family firms and how family firms, in turn, shape business families (James et al., 2012; Jaskiewicz et al., 2017b; Jaskiewicz & Dyer, 2017).

Research Opportunities. The perspective that considers family firms as a combination of family and business systems is reflected in the strong focus in the literature on governance structures and the reliance on agency theory. OT has been leveraged way less. Therefore, there are many interesting opportunities to explore. For instance:

- **RQs for Embedded Studies:**
  - *How do family firms strategically organize for hybridity?* *Large family firms comprise a portfolio of very different businesses, including investment offices and philanthropic ventures. How they can gain a competitive advantage from hybridity is an important question.
  - *How does the way family firms design their organization shape their strategies and behaviors?* *An organizational design perspective (De Massis et al., 2021) can shed light on how family firms' design choices shape their behaviors.
- **RQs for Integrative Studies:**
  - *How do theories of professional archetypes help us understand prevailing professionalization forms in family firms?* *As Salvato et al. (2019)

suggested, professionalization in family firm can be examined by integrating insights from archetype theory.

- *How do theories of family science change our understanding of corporate governance in family firms?* *Integrating the complexity of organizing the family, not just the business, can yield important insights about how the family shapes organizational choices.

- **RQs for Challenger Studies:**
  - *How does family involvement challenge/extend theories of categorization and the categorical imperative?* *Family firms must organize to adhere to the expectation of relevant audiences (e.g., analysts if publicly traded firms). How do these dynamics play out when the family component is added (Zuckerman, 1999)?
  - *How does family involvement challenge/extend theories of resource dependence and power?* *Resource dependence theory has been rarely drawn upon in the family business literature, but family firms can be very insightful because of the dependence among family members and other power dynamics (see Huang et al., 2020).

- **RQs for Generalized Studies:**
  - *How do organizations characterized by "intractable conflict" organize to avoid self-destruction?* *A family firm is an ideal setting to examine how organizations operate in a situation of conflict that is often intractable (i.e., long-term, recurrent, and without exit or dissolution as a solution).

4.2 Mastering Tensions, Dualities, and Paradoxes

In the OT literature, theories of tensions, dualities, and paradoxes are rapidly gaining traction (Smith & Lewis, 2022). Although paradoxical thinking has a long tradition, organizational scholars have relatively recently refocused attention to these paradigms. Embracing paradoxical thinking has become particularly important in a world where resources are increasingly scarce and diverse demands more and more pressing (Smith et al., 2017). We highlight two streams of work that offer valuable insights: the growing community of researcher on paradox (Smith & Lewis, 2011) and the lens of optimal distinctiveness at the intersection of OT and strategy (Zhao, 2022).

Conversations and debates in the family business domain also highlight the challenges of strategically make decisions in the presence of tensions, dualities, ad paradoxes. These challenges emerge because the family and business systems interact in complex ways when it comes to value systems, preferences, and interests. From a strategic perspective this brings another layer of complexity to consider, which pertains to how hybridity affects strategic decision-making. Thus, a second key topic that particularly benefits from the dialogue between OT and FB research is *mastering tensions, dualities, and paradoxes*. The focus on this section is therefore the following:

Research Focus: (a) *How does research in family firms inform knowledge on tensions, dualities, and paradoxes in OT?* (b) *How does OT research advance knowledge on how family firms strategically master tensions, dualities, and paradoxes stemming from the complexity of managing multiple strategic dimensions and multiple different (internal and external) stakeholders?*

4.2.1 Theories of Paradoxes

As an organizational concept, paradox is defined as "contradictory yet interrelated elements that exist simultaneously and persist over time" (Smith & Lewis, 2011, p. 382). Attention to contradictions and tensions has always been strong in organizational thinking, for example, in the contingency approach (Lawrence & Lorsch, 1967; Poole & Van de Ven, 1989). However, early thinking emphasized the benefits of choosing among alternatives, whereas paradox thinking emphasizes the long-term benefits for organizations to attend to competing demands simultaneously. Starting with the work of Smith and Lewis (2011), research on paradoxes has achieved a more cohesive understanding, and scholars have coalesced around this approach to create a more unified paradox community. Among the several important insights of this review of the literature, we highlight two elements. First, the useful categorization of paradoxes into four groups provided by these authors: learning (knowledge), belonging (identity/interpersonal relationships), organizing (processes), and performing (goals). Learning paradoxes refer to dynamics of change, innovation, and renewal; belonging paradoxes are about tensions between identities; organizing paradoxes refer to competing designs and processes to achieve a desired outcome; and performing paradoxes refer to tensions from differing, conflicting demands of varied internal and external stakeholders.

Second, the insight about strategies to manage these paradoxes through acceptance or resolution. Specifically, four strategic responses are identified in the literature (based on Poole & Van de Ven, 1989): (1) acceptance, which means to keep tensions separate and appreciate their differences; (2) spatial separation, allocating opposing forces across different organizational units; (3) temporal separation, choosing one pole of a tension at one point in time and then switching; and (4) synthesis, seeking a view that accommodates the opposing poles.

To approach this topic, we recommend the Special Issue in *Organization Studies* on "Paradox, tensions, and dualities of innovation and change" and the introduction by the guest editors (Smith et al., 2017). As the authors note, "interdependencies of opposing elements have been recognized in this work, but much of the nuance and complexity that characterize these interdependencies remains unexamined or under-theorized" (Smith et al., 2017, p. 306). Family businesses are characterized by elements that can be in opposition and are inherently interdependent. Hence, there are a lot of opportunities for dialogue between these two streams of work.

Tensions, Dualities, and Paradoxes in the FB Literature. We are clearly not the first to see the benefits of this line of thinking (see Ingram et al., 2016; Zellweger, 2017), but we suggest that insights from prior work need further elaboration and discussion to inform the current scholarly conversation. We look at two paradoxes that are particularly salient in family firms. First, the equal importance – and associated tensions – between financial and nonfinancial goals (performing paradox). Second, scholars have drawn on paradoxical thinking to examine the theme of innovation in family firms. Specifically, scholars have examined ambidexterity (learning paradox), but also the tension between past and tradition and innovation for the future (belonging paradox). We review and discuss this line of research in the following paragraphs. The lens of paradox, we argue, provides an excellent source of insights on how family firms walk the "strategic tightrope" and can be successful doing it.

Managing Financial and Nonfinancial Goals. The equal importance of financial and nonfinancial goals is one of the key elements on which scholars have predicated the distinctiveness of family firms compared to nonfamily firms. This argument is at the core of the SEW approach (Gomez-Mejia et al., 2007, 2011), an extension of behavioral agency theory (Wiseman & Gomez-Mejia, 1998) that represents one, if not, the most commonly used framework to analyze strategies and behaviors of family firms (Berrone et al., 2012). This theoretical model predicts that firms make choices depending on the reference point of the firm's dominant principals (i.e., the family). Hence, family firms base their decisions on both economically logical rationales to increase financial wealth *and* noneconomical rationales, based on their desire to preserve and increase affective endowments. SEW is a decision-making logic that is not driven by efficiency or financial sense, but an economical logic of choice driven by five key dimensions, called FIBER. FIBER stands for Family control and influence (F), Identification of family members with the firm (I), Binding social ties (B), Emotional attachment of family members (E), and Renewal of family bonds to the firm through dynastic succession (R) (Gomez-Mejia et al., 2011).

The SEW perspective is still the most common framework to examine the multiplicity and the trade-off among goals in the family business literature. Later elaborations have included in the theory elements of prospect theory, mixed-gamble theory, and social psychology (see Jiang et al., 2018; Swab et al., 2020 for recent reviews). Interestingly, family business scholars highlight how the specific and direct focus on goals in these organizations is a relatively recent accomplishment. After a seminal paper by Tagiuri and Davis (1996), the topic of goals apparently fell in a memory-hole. The lack of research on the goals of family firms is indeed considered to be one of the most striking gaps in the literature (Debicki et al., 2009; Kotlar & De Massis, 2013). Building on the recent review by Vazquez and Rocha (2018), we highlight four areas of research on goals. Two of them explicitly investigate the paradoxical nature and trade-offs between goals. Specifically, these authors found a cluster of papers related to goal *content*. This line of work refers to the nature of the goals as either economic or noneconomic (Chrisman et al., 2003b; Debicki et al., 2009). A second cluster of papers examines goals *interaction*, by looking at how goals relate to each other – whether they are in trade-offs or integrated (Gedajlovic et al., 2012; Moores, 2009; Zellweger & Nason, 2008). The other two research clusters are concerned with goal recipients, in terms of stakeholders who benefit from the accomplishment of these goals (Sharma, 2004; Zellweger & Nason, 2008) and the goal setting or formulation process (Chrisman et al., 2003b; Debicki et al., 2009).

We discuss in more detail the first two clusters, because these papers offer insights into the key issue of how the goals of family firms interact with one another and whether they are perceived as paradoxical in family firms. Notably, scholarly work on goal content has been mostly descriptive thus far. Scholars appreciate that goal diversity is one of the key features of family firms (Carney, 2005). The pursuit of nonfinancial goals clearly suggests that understanding family firms requires to move beyond traditional economic theory based on shareholder wealth maximization (Zellweger et al., 2013). Most of the studies in this stream of research go on in classifying the goals of family firms in dichotomous pairs, thus reinforcing the idea that goals are in trade-offs with one another. Categories of goals include pecuniary versus nonpecuniary (e.g., Stockmans et al., 2010), economic versus noneconomic (e.g., Hauck et al., 2016), family centered versus business centered (e.g., Chrisman et al., 2014), financial versus nonfinancial (e.g., Minichilli et al., 2014), wealth creators versus value generators (e.g., Chrisman et al., 2003a), family support oriented versus economically oriented (e.g., Jaskiewicz & Luchak, 2013), and intrinsic or internal versus extrinsic or external (McKenny et al., 2012).

The second cluster of studies on goal interaction speaks more directly to the relationship between these goals. In this regard, scholars have looked at this interaction as a complex one, which typically involves trade-offs. From this perspective, the typical insight is that economical (or business centered) goals are at odds with noneconomical (or family-centered) goals. For example, Chrisman et al. (2014) provided a conceptual economic analysis to explain the motivations that influence the choice by family owners to hire family or nonfamily managers and decide the compensation of the firm's management team. The preference for family managers is a function of a complex set of factors, including economic and noneconomic goals. Other studies have adopted the same perspective, to highlight how the pursuit of family-centered nonfinancial goals may prevent family firms from fully exploiting economic opportunities (Feldman et al., 2016), represent a sacrifice of firms' wealth in the form of higher Initial Public Offering (IPO) underpricing (Leitterstorf & Rau, 2014), create agency costs at the expense of other goals (Stewart & Hitt, 2012) and constraints on resources (Chrisman et al., 2003a). Along this line of reasoning, Chrisman et al. discussed in a recent publication (2021) how the relational complexities and the presence of noneconomic goals are further exacerbated in multifamily firms (MFFs) owned and managed not by a single, but a small number of families. These authors highlight the agency problems that organizations encounter because of the divergence between family-centered noneconomic goals. They suggest that the survival of the business-owning families may be at risk. Interestingly, this Element offers governance mechanisms as possible solutions, in the form of mutual monitoring and contract renegotiations. Indeed, although the issue of conflicting, paradoxical goals is widely acknowledged, there seems to be a relative lack of studies on how to manage the challenges arising from paradoxical goals. It seems that most studies have adopted the point of view that resolution is unlikely, and an acceptance strategy is the best course of action to minimize disturbances and challenges.

Constructive insights in this direction come from the smaller cluster of studies that appreciate the complex, paradoxical nature of goals in family firms, and attempt to examine their potentially synergistic nature. For example, Zellweger and Nason (2008) use a stakeholder theory approach to deepen our understanding of financial and nonfinancial performance outcomes in family firms across multiple stakeholder categories. Similarly, other studies look at "goal ambidexterity" (Kammerlander et al., 2015), and, more generally, suggest that there is a possibility for goal congruence (Chrisman & Patel, 2012) and synergistic and symbiotic relationship between the family and the business (Chua et al., 2003). This is also the message of Vazquez and Rocha (2018), the authors of a review article on goals. The dichotomous view of goals is intrinsically tied to the use of theoretical frameworks like agency theory, and the tendency of scholars to use dichotomous classifications that put goals in antithesis with one another. As they propose, a way to rectify this is to extend the motivational and rational assumptions of agency theory (Rocha & Ghoshal, 2006) to focus on the unifying concept of value creation (as the unifying purpose that describes the content of goals), as well as on harmonization (as the main goal interaction mechanism). This is clearly a call to extend the theoretical breath of family business research to include a paradox lens and embrace some of the resolution strategies suggested in this line of research. As we discuss in the next section, the innovation literature has started to heed this call. The growing literature on organizational paradoxes stresses the potentially powerful relationships between paradoxes and innovation (e.g., Andriopoulos & Lewis, 2010; Gotsi et al., 2010). Scholars like Ingram et al. (2016) have also begun to create a bridge with the family business literature, by developing valid and reliable measures of paradoxical tensions and paradoxical thinking in innovation through an online survey of family firm executives.

Ambidexterity, Innovation, and the Balance with Tradition. Organizational ambidexterity is defined in the strategy innovation literature as the concern over how organizations can achieve the benefits of "exploitation" and "exploration," typically portrayed as incompatible learning processes (for a review, see Lavie et al., 2010). Exploitation focuses on quality and efficiency, enabling firms to closely monitor and optimize their current business activities. Exploration focuses on new opportunities about products, services, markets, and customers that allow firms to achieve long-term competitiveness (Goel & Jones III, 2016; O'Reilly III & Tushman, 2013; Raisch & Birkinshaw, 2008). In the family business domain, the study of ambidexterity belongs to a broader conversation about innovation (Kammerlander et al., 2020). In the following, we briefly summarize what is known about ambidexterity in family firms, and specifically, the role of family involvement on this strategic behavior. We then broaden the conversation to expand the vantage point to show how scholars have pointed as the balancing of innovation and tradition from the lens of "paradoxical cognitive frames" (Smith & Tushman, 2005) and "paradoxical challenges" (Jansen et al., 2009).

Even though organizational ambidexterity is considered as important for family firms as for nonfamily firms (McAdam et al., 2020; Miller & Le Breton-Miller, 2006), this line of research is relatively recent (e.g., Allison et al., 2014; Moss et al., 2014). Emerging studies often provide mixed evidence and findings. As often is the case, family business scholars consider that the peculiarities of family firms in terms of resources, goals, and structures make them substantially different from their nonfamily counterparts. For instance, a quote reported in Kammerlander et al. (2020) refer to explorative empirical evidence that suggests how "family firms apply ambidexterity in a completely different way than do their [nonfamily] counterparts" (Röd, 2016, p. 198, referring to Weismeier-Sammer, 2014). A large body of work that explores these differences, however, is not available yet. The intuition of family business scholars – and their consequent empirical efforts – have been focused on understanding how family involvement in top management affects organizational ambidexterity. Results are mixed and, at times, inconclusive. For instance, the relationship between family member involvement and organizational ambidexterity is reported as both positive (Stubner et al., 2012) and negative (Hiebl, 2015). Studies report a positive influence of nonfamily management on organizational ambidexterity (Röd, 2016; Veider & Matzler, 2016). The study by Kammerlander et al. (2020) brings some clarity by exploring family-specific antecedents of organizational ambidexterity, thus elucidating that family firms themselves are heterogeneous in the way they approach this behavior. These scholars show that top management composition (the share of family executives in top management) matters; critically, the relationship between top management team and ambidexterity is nonlinear (U-shaped) with an important moderating effect of family business goals. In short, there is a lot more to study about the extent and the modalities in which family firms engage in this behavior. Research questions abound as to whether family firms differ from nonfamily firms, the family-focused and organizational-focused antecedents, and the factors underlining the heterogenous approaches to ambidexterity by different family firms.

For us, the specific behavior of ambidexterity is just one instance of the paradoxical nature of strategic decision-making in family firms. One of the most exciting developments in family business research is the growing attention to the topic of innovation (Calabrò et al., 2019; Dieleman & Koning, 2019; Fuetsch & Suess-Reyes, 2017; Röd, 2016). Debunking commonly held assumptions about family firms' entrenched conservativism, family firms are emerging as a large portion of the world's most innovative firms (Kammerlander & van Essen, 2017). A growing body of literature has begun to show a more heterogenous and compelling picture (Chrisman et al., 2015; De Massis et al., 2015). Family firms are neither insensitive to the criticality of innovation to increase their likelihood of surviving across generations (Ingram et al., 2016; Jaskiewicz et al., 2015; Zellweger et al., 2012b) nor are they reluctant to embrace innovative behaviors to remain competitive in an increasingly complex world (Autio et al., 2014). Importantly, scholars have been motivated to solve the apparent paradox between the tendency of family firms to be conservative, risk averse, and less innovative (Chen & Hsu, 2009; Morris, 1998; Vago, 2004) and the recent evidence that family firms value the engagement in innovative activities (e.g., R&D and new product development (NPD)).

The contributions of this line of work can be summarized into two main streams. First, research shows that there are important differences in innovation indicators and behaviors between family and nonfamily business (Chrisman & Patel, 2012). Some studies have focused on how and why characteristics of family firms, such as flexible structures and decision-making processes and less formal monitoring and control (Daily & Dollinger, 1992; Geeraerts, 1984; Zahra et al., 2008), may support innovation (Craig & Dibrell, 2006; Özsomer et al., 1997). Scholars have also examined the idiosyncrasies of family firms and compared innovation input and innovation output, leading to the conclusion that family firms invest less in innovation but are more efficient in transforming innovation input into innovation output (De Massis et al., 2018b; Duran et al., 2016).

To better explain the ability-willingness paradox (Chrisman et al., 2015) – according to which have relative higher ability to innovate but less willingness to do so – other studies have examined not whether family firms innovate (i.e., drivers) and to what extent (i.e., innovation indicators), but how they do so. Examinations have shown the innovation processes and activities that family firms engage in, thus beginning to shed light on the heterogeneity of strategic orientations of family firms to innovation (Calantone & Rubera, 2012). A key insight is the idea that family firms differ in their "innovation postures" based on the risk-taking propensity and attachment to tradition (Rondi et al., 2019), and adopt strategies to manage the tradition-innovation paradox (Erdogan et al., 2020). Differently from the literature on competing goals – that emphasizes a trade-off over an integration perspective – these studies explicitly address the question: How do family firms manage the paradox between tradition and innovation? As these authors note, "in long-established family firms endowed with tradition bequests and doomed to renewal, an either/or approach to tradition and innovation is detrimental" (Erdogan et al., 2020, p. 23). Their qualitative findings based on a sample of long-lasting family firms in craft Turkish industries reveal that companies may choose different strategies based on their approach to tradition (i.e., revival vs. preservation) and innovation (i.e., segregation vs integration): protecting the heritage, maintaining the essence, embracing nostalgia, and restoring the legacy. These strategies echo and nuance some of the responses described in the paradox literature. Importantly, this study suggests that a synthesis approach may be the most suitable for family firms. The theoretical concept of temporal symbiosis encapsulates this message, by defining an organization's "simultaneous adoption of retrospective and prospective approaches to using its resources to concurrently perpetuate tradition and achieve innovation." A similar line of reasoning characterizes the recent interest of family business scholars in the strategic use of past and history (De Massis et al., 2016; Ge et al., 2022; Sasaki et al., 2019). From this vantage point, the past is a relatively malleable rhetorical resource that can be used by organizational leaders to manage paradoxes and even use them in a strategically advantageous way (Kroeze & Keulen, 2013; Suddaby et al., 2010). This theme overlaps to some extent with the last section of this section, where we examine another paradox typical of family firms – the criticality of modeling the present to support the long-term viability of the firm (and the family) in the future.

4.2.2 Optimal Distinctiveness

Optimal distinctiveness is a theoretical lens rooted in the work of Brewer (1991), who pioneered this line of research in social psychology, and Deephouse (1999), who extended the idea to the organizational level to propose strategic balance theory in institutional theory. Optimal distinctiveness is used to account for the issue organizations face because of the simultaneous pressure to be similar and different from their peers (Deephouse, 1999; Zhao et al., 2017; Zuckerman, 2016). Being perceived as similar, familiar, and compliant with normative industry expectations allows organizations to "blend in" and benefit from recognition and social benefits. However, being perceived as different increases the chances to "stand out" from the crowd and secure competitive advantage. Organizations perceive these competing pressures, and this stream of work has been particularly attentive to understand how organizations can balance the two to find an optimal point in their competitive positioning.

Like the literature on paradoxes, scholars have initially focused on conformity and differentiation as two opposing poles to conceptualize this tension (grounded in the disciplinary traditions of institutional theory and strategic management respectively). Relatively recently, the framework has been revamped in a theoretical domain at the intersection of OT and strategy (see Zhao, 2022). Importantly, Zhao et al. have revised the idea of optimal distinctiveness to include the possibility that opposing poles may be enabling, and not just in a relationship of trade-offs. Optimal distinctiveness is being reframed from a "static positioning point on a single organizational dimension" to a "dynamic process whereby organizations, viewed as complex and multidimensional entities, identify and orchestrate various types of strategic resources and actions to reconcile the conformity versus differentiation tension, address the multiplicity of stakeholder expectations, and aptly modify their positioning strategies in order to succeed in multilevel and dynamic environments."

The framework has a long tradition and has generated many insights when applied to domains in strategy, entrepreneurship, and international management. Thus far, optimal distinctiveness has been mostly studied in quantitative papers, and to our knowledge it has been used very rarely in the family business domain. One exception is the paper by Miller et al. (2018), where the authors explored strategic distinctiveness in listed and private family firms. Listed family firms are quite interesting because of their unorthodox ownership structure. Findings reveal that the nature of the ownership shapes the degree of conformity, with listed family firms conforming more to the industry strategic financial norms; the relationship of conformity to performance depends on ownership and governance but also on the strategic orchestration of multiple dimensions of strategy.

4.2.3 Research Opportunities

Even though the family business literature recognizes the complexity of dualities and contradictions in family firms, concepts and theories from OT have not been leveraged or integrated consistently in this domain. Concepts from the FB domain are also underutilized, as are family firms as empirical settings for advancing theory. The paradox lens and the optimal distinctiveness lens are highly relatable in their approaches and methodologically complementary. In fact, there is a striking prevalence of qualitative studies in the paradox lens applied to organization studies (Smith et al., 2017); conversely, there is a prevalence of quantitative studies in the optimal distinctiveness domain (Zhao, 2022). We offer a few research ideas to further this direction of research. For instance:

- **RQs for Embedded Studies:**
  - *How do family firms develop paradoxical mindsets?* *Many organizations are trapped in trade-off mindsets, but family firms are used to think in terms of "and" rather than "or."
  - *How do family firms engage in categorical flexibility, moving between opposing poles when making strategic decisions about goals, investments, and innovation strategies?* *Paradoxical thinking (Calabretta et al., 2017) and categorical flexibility (Sharma & Bansal, 2017) are two examples of concepts from the paradox literature that can be fruitfully applied to research in the FB domain.
  - *What dimensions of optimal distinctiveness are most salient in family firms? Is this a relevant source of heterogeneity across these organizations?* *Optimal distinctiveness is under-researched in the family business domain

and exploratory studies may be necessary to understand the concept in this domain.

- **RQs for Integrative Studies:**
  - *How can theories of paradoxical tensions be integrated with succession frameworks to better understand succession in family firms?* *Succession is a key topic in the FB domain that is fraught with tensions and contradictions. Integrating theories of paradox *management* can help scholars reveal successful strategies and pitfalls.
  - *How do individuals make sense and frame paradoxical tension about innovation and tradition in family and nonfamily firms?* *Integrating theories of sensemaking and framing with paradox theories can yield insights into differences between groups (e.g., differences between family and nonfamily firms, different generations, family and nonfamily members, internal and external stakeholders etc.)
  - *How do family enterprises optimally position themselves and are categorized by external audiences as they grow and diversify?* *Integrating optimal distinctiveness with ecological dynamics and market categorization can help advance knowledge on the market category level.
- **RQs for Challenger Studies:**
  - *How does* SEW *challenge/extend theories of paradoxical thinking?* *Family firms are driven by SEW in their decisions; however, the theoretical relationship between SEW and paradoxes is not clear and needs exploration.
  - *How do theories of paradoxical mindsets in family firms challenge/expand agency and behavioral theoretical predictions?* *Agency and behavioral theories, as well as paradox theories, have emphasized the cognitive component. Examining paradoxes in family firms brings emotions and affect front and center.
  - *How do contextual contingencies (such as ownership as an organizational characteristic) alter general predictions about optimal distinctiveness?* *The family ownership variable could provide an important boundary condition to explain how family and nonfamily firms address tensions and orchestrate resources.
- **RQs for Generalized Studies:**
  - *How can theories of paradoxes accommodate trialectical relationships?* *Paradox theories remain constrained by their focus on two elements in direct opposition to one another. Family firms offer a setting with multiple opposing poles linked to ownership, management, family, and wealth. A study of a family firm could shed light on this issue.

- ○ *What role does identity play in the ability of an organization to embrace a paradoxical mindset?* *This is a question that could be addresses very effectively in a family firm.
- ○ *How does paradoxical thinking change with cultural mindsets?* *A comparative in-depth case study of family organizations would shed light on national culture as an important source of heterogeneity and advance cross-cultural theories of paradoxes.
- ○ *What are the mechanisms thought which an organization can achieve and leverage a synergy between conformity and differentiation?* *A family firm is an ideal setting to understand how such synergy is achieved and maintained because so many family businesses seem to be quite successful at doing this over a long period of time.

4.3 Modeling Time and Temporality

Time and temporality are intrinsically important variables in management research (Kunisch et al., 2017; Mosakowski & Earley, 2000). Yet, there has been relatively less interest in theorizing deeply about these variables. Until recently, OT scholars have primarily considered time and its dimensions (e.g., speed, temporal depth, horizon, and rhythm) as an "index against which processes are measured" (Reinecke & Lawrence, in press, p. 10). For instance, as a measure of change in pace (Amis et al., 2004; Lawrence et al., 2001), or as quantitative explanatory variables related to performance constructs (Bansal et al., 2022). Recently, however, there has been a stream of reinvigorated theoretical conversations around time and temporality in the OT domain. These new ideas have been driven by a growing interest in expanding the conceptualization of time and connecting it more strongly with process ontologies and history (Langley et al., 2013; Reinecke et al., 2021).

Along the same lines, time and temporality are core concepts to a domain of research that focuses on long-lasting, multigenerational organizations such as family businesses. Yet, rather surprisingly, temporal constructs have not been incorporated extensively in family business research (Sharma et al., 2014). The focus on this section is therefore the following:

Research Focus: (a) *How does research in family firms inform the way time and temporality have been examined and modeled in OT research?* (b) *How does OT research advance knowledge on how family firms perceive, interpret, and model time and temporality to achieve transgenerational sustainability?*

4.3.1 Time and Temporality in OT Research

A review of the literature on time and temporality is outside the scope of this Element, but it is useful to consider a few concepts and insights from this stream of work to examine potential fruitful connections between the field of OT and FB.

Process Studies. First, one key point emerging from the OT literature is that organizational life and social structures have an inherent temporal structure that can be revealed by adopting a process ontology. Process research "focuses empirically on evolving phenomena, and it draws on theorizing that explicitly incorporates temporal progressions of activities as elements of explanation and understanding" (Langley et al., 2013, p. 1). The Special Research Forum on "Process studies of change in organization and management" published in the *Academy of Management Journal* in 2013 encouraged scholars to dive into the complexity of process studies and explore how managerial and organizational phenomena emerge, change, and unfold over time. All the papers in the Special Issue focused on temporally evolving phenomena and reveal the need to obtain longitudinal data (whether obtained with archival, historical, or real-time field observations) to observe how processes unfold over time.

Temporal Work. A second, important contribution emerging from the ongoing conversation in OT (at the intersection with strategy) is the concept of "temporal work." The term was introduced by Kaplan and Orlikowski (2013) to describe the collective alignment of organizational members' conceptions of past, present, and future to develop strategic projects. Later on, institutional scholars used the same concept to explain how actors can exploit windows of opportunity and temporal norms to drive change processes (Granqvist & Gustafsson, 2016). In a similar vein, the recognition that temporal work may influence and shape interpretation, and not just align them, invited scholars to redefine temporal work as the "any individual, collective or organizational effort to influence, sustain or redirect the temporal assumptions or patterns that shape strategic action" (Bansal et al., 2022, p. 7). In the 2022 Special Issue of *Strategic Organization* devoted to "Temporal work: The strategic organization of time," the editors found that the published papers developed two conceptual themes: one explored the targets of temporal work (the *what* question), and the other explored the media or mechanisms of temporal work (the *how* question). Targets for temporal work include shaping temporal perceptions and interpretations, shaping temporal structures, and shaping temporal values; media for temporal work include temporal talk, temporal practices, and temporal objects.

This Special Issue is just one of the several initiatives that reveal the renewed interest in themes of time, temporality, and history in strategy and OT (Argyres et al., 2020; Bansal et al., 2022; Reinecke et al., 2021).

Process Ontology and Institutions. A third, boundary-pushing, conversation that is flourishing in the institutional domain considers time and temporality as core concepts to redefine "institutions" and institutional processes (Meyer, 2019; Reay et al., 2019; Weik, 2019). Specifically, what is being challenged is the understanding of institutions as stable and enduring social structures. The new conceptualization that is offered is grounded in a process ontology and suggests that institutions are "the unfolding outcome of people's and collective actors' continual efforts to maintain, modify, or disturb them" (Reay et al., 2019, p. 1). From this vantage point, institutions are not "fixed" objects; they are continuously in flux and "ever-becoming yet enduring social processes that are meaningful and carry prescriptions for actors' legitimate participation in them" (Reinecke & Lawrence, in press, p. 9). Notably, Reinecke and Lawrence (in press) encourage institutional scholars to complement studies of temporal work in the context of change, building on the idea that temporality underpins institutional stabilization as well. In their view, temporality affects meanings, prescriptions, and participation as key elements of institutions. The authors provide a wide array of useful concepts-related temporality – temporal patterns, expectancies, and mechanisms – and explain their role in shaping institutional components.

4.3.2 Time and Temporality in FB Research

In 2011, Sharma et al. issue a call for paper for a Special Issue in *Family Business Review* on "Temporal dimensions of family enterprise research." The editors noted that studies that "explicitly incorporate time-related variables in family business research are exceptions rather than the norm" (Sharma et al., 2014, p. 10). Specifically, research seemed to coalesce around time-related variables: family firms' long-term orientation (LTO; Le Breton–Miller & Miller, 2006; Lumpkin et al., 2010), organizational survival or longevity (e.g., Colli, 2012; Fahed-Sreih & Djoundourian, 2006; Sharma & Salvato, 2013), and transgenerational entrepreneurship (Habbershon et al., 2010). We briefly review these concepts.

Long-term Orientation, Succession, and Transgenerational Entrepreneurship. A long-term perspective has been identified early on as one of the idiosyncratic attributes that distinguish family from nonfamily firms and shape their strategic behavior (Dodd et al., 2013; Miller & Le Breton-Miller, 2005). Long-term orientation refers to "the tendency to prioritize the long-range implications and impact of decisions and actions that come to fruition after an extended time period" (Lumpkin et al., 2010, p. 241). Because family businesses are interested in the survival and success of the business across generations and consider important to create a legacy and lasting values (Ward, 2004), FB scholars concluded that family enterprises are more likely to be long-term oriented than nonfamily firms (Gomez-Mejia et al., 2007; Kellermanns et al., 2008). Research on this topic has focused on understanding how such long-term perspectives influence strategic choices, such as the risk of investments (Zellweger, 2007), internationalization (Zahra, 2003), and innovation (Diaz-Moriana et al., 2020). In general, the common understanding is that the way family firms perceive time may yield potential advantages and benefits. There is, however, a debate whether family firms are more long-term oriented or control-oriented, and their decisions are more influenced by the desire to retain control, rather than preserving the organization for future generations (Chrisman & Patel, 2012).

The issue of time has been further examined in the context of succession. Succession is a topic that has attracted much research interest and lots of ink in the family business field. Considerable efforts have been made to better understand continuity and succession as well as how existing business is perpetuated (e.g., Le Breton–Miller et al., 2004). Early research tended to focus on the difficulties, challenges, and trade-offs of this process (Ingram et al., 2016; Radu-Lefebvre & Randerson, 2020). Indeed, intergenerational succession remains a problematic issue for family firms (De Massis et al., 2008) and our knowledge about "generations" is still selective and limited (Magrelli et al., 2022b). The next generation is often ignored and neglected in current studies (Jaskiewicz & Rau, 2021). Either it is considered inadequate to keep the entrepreneurial spirit of the founding generation (Zahra et al., 2008) or depicted as not interested in taking over their parents' businesses (Zellweger et al., 2011).

Recently, however, this conventional approach is being reconsidered and revisited (Habbershon et al., 2010). The increasing focus on entrepreneurial mindsets in the family business field has created a new line of thinking about what succession is and what matters the most. Specifically, the focus of analysis is no longer the struggle to pass on a business across generations, but the idea that family firms are "enterprising families," that is, business families that strive for transgenerational entrepreneurship and long-term wealth creation through the creation of new ventures, innovation, and strategic renewal (Habbershon & Pistrui, 2002). There is a growing body of work on transgenerational entrepreneurship, which is defined as "the processes through which a family uses and develops entrepreneurial mindsets and family influenced resources and capabilities to create new streams of entrepreneurial, financial and social value across generations" (Habbershon et al., 2010, p. 1).

Overall, studies on time in the FB domain are not focused specifically on temporal dynamics. The focus has been mostly on longitudinal examination of strategies or processes over time, for instance, exploration/exploitation (Allison et al., 2014), proactiveness (De Massis et al., 2014), and entrepreneurial business models (Clinton et al., 2018). Theorizing about time dimensions, perceptions of time and temporality is still pushed in the background. One notable exception is the paper by Magrelli et al. (2022a), published in the *Strategic Organization* Special Issue mentioned earlier. The study puts orientations toward the past, present, and future at the center of the mediation process that helps family firms manage intergenerational tensions. As discovered by the authors, temporal work enables different generations to align their perceptions and interpretations of past, present, and future, creating a form of continuity. This is an example of a move in FB research to consider alternative facets of temporality from a historical point of view.

History, Past, and Entrepreneurial Legacies. A connected, yet distinct, body of work that encapsulates time and temporality is the one on history and entrepreneurial legacies, defined as "the family's rhetorical reconstruction of past entrepreneurial achievements or resilience" (Jaskiewicz et al., 2015, p. 29). This stream of research is less concerned with the issue of how family enterprises can thrive across generations. The focus is on how family firms' long-term view is embodied in their ability to embrace both the past and the future. For instance, Barbera et al. (2018) linked entrepreneurial legacies to storytelling by showing their fluid nature across time, as they are shaped and variously interpreted by different generations. This stream of family business research considers history as a key idiosyncratic component of family enterprises and therefore an important variable of theory or empirical analysis (Argyres et al., 2020; Sasaki et al., 2020; Sinha et al., 2020; Suddaby et al., 2020; Suddaby & Foster, 2017). The direction of growth in this line of work is in drawing a direct connection between family firms and their historical legacies. Specifically, scholars have begun to examine more directly the mechanisms linking family history to the creation of competitive advantage (Ge et al., 2022). Opportunities for theorizing abound, as FB research has only begun to scratch the surface on topics such as time and temporality.

4.3.3 Research Opportunities

As noted in this brief overview, the OT and FB research seem to have a relatively wider gap in terms of what has been interesting for scholars to explore. OT research has been focused on bringing to the fore the temporal aspects of process studies, suggesting that this lens can advance our thinking further. The FB research has been preoccupied with longevity, succession, entrepreneurial legacies and, more recently, with the use of rhetorical strategies about the past. We offer a few research ideas to narrow this gap and create areas for dialogue between the two fields. For instance:

- **RQs for Embedded Studies:**
  ◦ *How do internal and external stakeholders work to shape temporal patterns in family enterprises?* *Drawing on the temporal work framework can advance our (thus far) limited understanding of how time and its patterns are shaped in family firms.
  ◦ *How do temporal dimensions shape the succession processes?* *Studies of succession have focused on issues such as leadership, power transfer, conflict between generations, communication, and the existence or absence of a pre-defined plan stating the rules for succession (Porfírio et al., 2020).
  ◦ *What is the role of temporal dimensions (such as rhythm, patterns, speed) in ensuring a successful transition?* *Temporal dimensions are severely understudied.

- **RQs for Integrative Studies:**
  ◦ *How can temporality help us understand the ongoing stabilization of family firms as institutions?* *Family firms can become institutions (Sasaki et al., 2019) but this status is an ongoing accomplishment. Whereas we tend to ascribe changes in ownership, board, and management structure as primary drivers of whether a firm is deemed "family" or "non-family," the process perspective focused on temporality in the stabilization of institutions (Reinecke & Lawrence, in press) can reveal new insights on the sources of longevity of long-lasting family organizations.
  ◦ *How does historical legacy and strategic use of the past enable the mainten- ance of a family identity when there is no longer family intervention in management or ownership?* *Integrating identity theory and legacies can shed light on the maintenance of OI in firms that are no longer family firms.

- **RQs for Challenger Studies:**
  ◦ *How does a process ontology and time dimensions connect to the FIBER dimensions of SEW?* * SEW is a key concept in FB research but its applicability has been debated. The FIBER dimensions have an intrinsic temporal component that, if explored, can inform the way we think about temporality and provide a new fresh outlook to the SEW framework.

- **RQs for Generalized Studies:**
  ◦ *How does organizational members' encoding of the past and/or future (for instance, in terms of past nostalgia or future hopes and dreams) animates*

participation in certain institutional arrangements? *This question directly speaks the role of participation in institutional stabilization. It can be addressed quite effectively in a family firm, where these dynamics are very salient.

5 Concluding Thoughts

We started this Element with the puzzling question of how and why OT and FB research are just partially integrated fields and, even further, asking ourselves why they are two separate fields in the first place. Looking back at the origin of OT (Hinings & Meyer, 2018) it is reasonable to assume that family businesses were equally (if not more) prevalent in the economic landscape in the geographical and temporal frame when OT started to emerge. Moreover, the family was an institution at the core of the emergence of large corporations in the United States and still represents the backbone of small and medium-sized businesses in Europe. While an interesting question to ponder, it remains a fact that OT and FB have developed on parallel paths and these two scholarly communities have just begun to have consistent and constructive interactions. There is also a trend in FB scholarship to draw on theoretical perspectives in the strategy field (e.g., behavioral agency theory) that have become the foundation of the FB domain. Conversely, engagement with OT is sporadic, driven by the work of a small group of scholars. The first author of this Element is fortunate to belong to this group of scholars who have enjoyably straddled the two fields. There are many benefits and opportunities arising from interacting with both audiences, with occasional challenges stemming from joining conversations "out of turn" or not always being in synch with the theoretical flow of each community.

This Element has the ambition of widening the space for dialogue between OT and FB scholarships. We are not the first to make this call (and we won't be the last probably), but the time seems ripe to renew this proposition. We build on the efforts and the achievements attained by other forward-looking scholars before us who have created places for dialogue and interaction through special issues, conferences, and other means. What we have sought to achieve is to build on the strengths of both fields, highlighting their respective accomplishments and areas of development to introduce the two audiences to one another. There are several sources that summarize the origin and development of OT better than us, so we have limited our coverage on that topic. We have also purposefully avoided considering the "family firm" just as an empirical context. Instead, we offer a 2 × 2 framework that allows us to engage different audiences and discuss different rules of engagement between OT and FB. Scholars can draw on OT frameworks to address a research question that is specific to family enterprises. However, there is an opportunity to develop more complex and reciprocal interactions.

To this end, we have selected three areas of dialogue and fleshed out opportunities for multiple conversations. The research foci we discuss – managing hybridity, mastering tensions, dualities and paradoxes, and modeling time and temporalities – are at different levels of convergence. Hybridity has grown as a theoretical lens in OT and is grounded in established paradigms such as logics, identities, and organizational forms. These frameworks and ideas have been already used in prior works in the FB field. Thus, we have zoomed in on some concepts and suggested ways in which OT and FB scholars are invited to integrate these insights. The understanding of dualities and paradoxes and optimal distinctiveness in the OT arena is rapidly growing and holds great promise to address challenges that appear intractable. We see valuable opportunities for reciprocal learning between OT and FB in the context of understanding and leveraging on the synergic, rather than opposing, potentialities of tensions and contradictions. Family business research has just begun to embrace paradoxical thinking, so there are numerous paths of theorizing in this direction. Finally, time and temporality are relatively emerging perspectives in both OT and FB. Scholars are still coalescing around some key temporal dimensions and examine how they affect organizational processes and social structures. In this domain, FB and OT research is developing in specific areas of interest and there is a possibility to start a dialogue in the early phase of theoretical development.

Our hope is that this Element will be informative and thought-provoking for a wide array of audiences. We hope it will spark the curiosity of our readers, gently poke some assumptions, and act as a broker to create new connections and theoretical conversations.

References

Abdelgawad, S. G., & Zahra, S. A. (2020). Family firms' religious identity and strategic renewal. *Journal of Business Ethics*, *163*(4), 775–87.

Adler, P. S. (2001). Market, hierarchy, and trust: The knowledge economy and the future of capitalism. *Organization Science*, *12*(2), 215–34.

Aguilera, R. V., & Crespi-Cladera, R. (2012). Firm family firms: Current debates of corporate governance in family firms. *Journal of Family Business Strategy*, *3*(2), 66–69.

Ainsworth, S., & Cox, J. W. (2003). Families divided: Culture and control in small family business. *Organization Studies*, *24*(9), 1463–85.

Akhmedova, A., Cavallotti, R., Marimon, F., & Campopiano, G. (2020). Daughters' careers in family business: Motivation types and family-specific barriers. *Journal of Family Business Strategy*, *11*(3), 100307.

Albert, S. (1998). The definition and metadefinition of identity. In D. A. Whetten & P. C. Godfrey (Eds.), *Identity in organizations: Building theory through conversations* (pp. 1–13). Sage Publications Inc.

Albert, S., & Adams, E. (2002). The hybrid identity of law firms. In B. Moingeon & G. Soenen (Eds.) *Corporate and organizational identities* (pp. 55–70). Routledge.

Albert, S., & Whetten, D. A. (1985). Organizational identity. *Research in Organizational Behavior*, *7*, 263–95.

Aldrich, H. E., & Cliff, J. E. (2003). The pervasive effects of family on entrepreneurship: Toward a family embeddedness perspective. *Journal of Business Venturing*, *18*(5), 573–96.

Allison, T. H., McKenny, A. F., & Short, J. C. (2014). Integrating time into family business research: Using random coefficient modeling to examine temporal influences on family firm ambidexterity. *Family Business Review*, *27*(1), 20–34.

Almandoz, J. (2012). Arriving at the starting line: The impact of community and financial logics on new banking ventures. *Academy of Management Journal*, *55*(6), 1381–406.

Amis, J., Slack, T., & Hinings, C. R. (2004). The pace, sequence, and linearity of radical change. *Academy of Management Journal*, *47*(1), 15–39.

Anderson, R. C., & Reeb, D. M. (2004). Board composition: Balancing family influence in S&P 500 firms. *Administrative Science Quarterly*, *49*(2), 209–37.

Andriopoulos, C., & Lewis, M. W. (2010). Managing innovation paradoxes: Ambidexterity lessons from leading product design companies. *Long Range Planning*, *43*(1), 104–22.

Ansari, I. F., Goergen, M., & Mira, S. (2014). The determinants of the CEO successor choice in family firms. *Journal of Corporate Finance*, *28*, 6–25.

Anteby, M., & Wrzesniewski, A. (2014). In search of the self at work: Young adults' experiences of a dual identity organization. In H. R. Greve & M.-d. L. Seidel (Eds.) *Adolescent experiences and adult work outcomes: Connections and causes (Research in the Sociology of Work, Vol. 25*, pp. 13–50). Emerald Group.

Argyres, N. S., De Massis, A., Foss, N. J. et al. (2020). History-informed strategy research: The promise of history and historical research methods in advancing strategy scholarship. *Strategic Management Journal*, *41*(3), 343–68.

Arregle, J. L., Hitt, M. A., Sirmon, D. G., & Very, P. (2007). The development of organizational social capital: Attributes of family firms. *Journal of Management Studies*, *44*(1), 73–95.

Arzubiaga, U., Kotlar, J., De Massis, A., Maseda, A., & Iturralde, T. (2018). Entrepreneurial orientation and innovation in family SMEs: Unveiling the (actual) impact of the Board of Directors. *Journal of Business Venturing*, *33*(4), 455–69.

Ashforth, B. E., & Reingen, P. H. (2014). Functions of dysfunction: Managing the dynamics of an organizational duality in a natural food cooperative. *Administrative Science Quarterly*, *59*(3), 474–516.

Astrachan, J. H., Klein, S. B., & Smyrnios, K. X. (2002). The F-PEC scale of family influence: A proposal for solving the family business definition problem. *Family Business Review*, *15*(1), 45–58.

Autio, E., Kenney, M., Mustar, P., Siegel, D., & Wright, M. (2014). Entrepreneurial innovation: The importance of context. *Research Policy*, *43*(7), 1097–108.

Bansal, P., Reinecke, J., Suddaby, R., & Langley, A. (2022). Temporal work: The strategic organization of time. *Strategic Organization*, *20*(1), 6–19.

Barbera, F., Stamm, I., & DeWitt, R. L. (2018). The development of an entrepreneurial legacy: Exploring the role of anticipated futures in transgenerational entrepreneurship. *Family Business Review*, *31*(3), 352–78.

Basco, R. (2013). The family's effect on family firm performance: A model testing the demographic and essence approaches. *Journal of Family Business Strategy*, *4*(1), 42–66.

Basco, R., & Pérez Rodríguez, M. J. (2009). Studying the family enterprise holistically: Evidence for integrated family and business systems. *Family Business Review*, *22*(1), 82–95.

Battilana, J., Besharov, M., & Mitzinneck, B. (2017). On hybrids and hybrid organizing: A review and roadmap for future research. In R. Greenwood, C. Oliver, T. B. Lawrence, & R. E. Meyer (Eds.), *The SAGE handbook of organizational institutionalism* (2nd ed., pp. 133–69). Sage.

Battilana, J., & Dorado, S. (2010). Building sustainable hybrid organizations: The case of commercial microfinance organizations. *Academy of Management Journal, 53*(6), 1419–440.

Battilana, J., & Lee, M. (2014). Advancing research on hybrid organizing: Insights from the study of social enterprises. *Academy of Management Annals, 8*(1), 397–441.

Bengtson, V. L., & Achenbaum, W. A. (1993). *The changing contract across generations.* Transaction.

Berrone, P., Cruz, C., & Gomez-Mejia, L. R. (2012). Socioemotional wealth in family firms: Theoretical dimensions, assessment approaches, and agenda for future research. *Family Business Review, 25*(3), 258–79.

Berrone, P., Cruz, C., Gomez-Mejia, L. R., & Larraza-Kintana, M. (2010). Socioemotional wealth and corporate responses to institutional pressures: Do family-controlled firms pollute less? *Administrative Science Quarterly, 55*(1), 82–113.

Besharov, M. L., & Smith, W. K. (2014). Multiple institutional logics in organizations: Explaining their varied nature and implications. *Academy of Management Review, 39*(3), 364–81.

Bizri, R. (2016). Succession in the family business: Drivers and pathways. *International Journal of Entrepreneurial Behavior & Research, 22*(1), 133–54.

Blair, J. D., & Hunt, J. G. (1986). Getting inside the head of the management researcher one more time: Context-free and context-specific orientations in research. *Journal of Management, 12*(2), 147–66.

Boers, B., & Nordqvist, M. (2012). Understanding hybrid-identity organizations: The case of publicly listed family businesses. In A. Carsrud & M. Brännback, M. (Eds.), *Understanding family businesses* (pp. 251–69). Springer.

Bork, D., Jaffe, D. T., Lane, S. H., Dashew, L., & Heisler, Q. G. (1996). *Working with family businesses: A guide for professionals.* Jossey-Bass.

Borys, B., & Jemison, D. B. (1989). Hybrid arrangements as strategic alliances: Theoretical issues in organizational combinations. *Academy of Management Review, 14*(2), 234–49.

Brewer, M. B. (1991). The social self: On being the same and different at the same time. *Personality and Social Psychological Bulletin, 17*(5), 475–82.

Brinkerink, J., Rondi, E., Benedetti, C., & Arzubiaga, U. (2020). Family business or business family? Organizational identity elasticity and strategic responses to disruptive innovation. *Journal of Family Business Strategy, 11* (4), 100360.

Bruton, G. D., Peng, M. W., Ahlstrom, D., Stan, C., & Xu, K. (2015). State-owned enterprises around the world as hybrid organizations.*Academy of Management Perspectives*, *29*(1), 92–114.

Byrne, J., Radu-Lefebvre, M., Fattoum, S., & Balachandra, L. (2021). Gender gymnastics in CEO succession: Masculinities, femininities and legitimacy. *Organization Studies*, *42*(1), 129–59.

Cabeza-García, L., Sacristán-Navarro, M., & Gómez-Ansón, S. (2017). Family involvement and corporate social responsibility disclosure. *Journal of Family Business Strategy*, *8*(2), 109–22.

Calabretta, G., Gemser, G., & Wijnberg, N. M. (2017). The interplay between intuition and rationality in strategic decision making: A paradox perspective. *Organization Studies*, *38*(3–4), 365–401.

Calabrò, A., Torchia, M., Pukall, T., & Mussolino, D. (2013). The influence of ownership structure and board strategic involvement on international sales: The moderating effect of family involvement. *International Business Review*, *22*(3), 509–23.

Calabrò, A., Vecchiarini, M., Gast, J. et al. (2019). Innovation in family firms: A systematic literature review and guidance for future research. *International Journal of Management Reviews*, *21*(3), 317–55.

Calantone, R., & Rubera, G. (2012). When should RD & E and marketing collaborate? The moderating role of exploration–exploitation and environmental uncertainty. *Journal of Product Innovation Management*, *29*(1), 144–57.

Cannella Jr, A. A., Jones, C. D., & Withers, M. C. (2015). Family-versus lone-founder-controlled public corporations: Social identity theory and boards of directors. *Academy of Management Journal*, *58*(2), 436–59.

Cappellaro, G., Tracey, P., & Greenwood, R. (2020). From logic acceptance to logic rejection: The process of destabilization in hybrid organizations. *Organization Science*, *31*(2), 415–38.

Carney, M. (2005). Corporate governance and competitive advantage in family-controlled firms. *Entrepreneurship Theory and Practice*, *29*(3), 249–65.

Carney, M., & Gedajlovic, E. (2002). The co-evolution of institutional environments and organizational strategies: The rise of family business groups in the ASEAN region. *Organization Studies*, *23*(1), 1–29.

Caselli, S., & Di Giuli, A. (2010). Does the CFO matter in family firms? Evidence from Italy. *European Journal of Finance*, *16*(5), 381–411.

Chadwick, I. C., & Dawson, A. (2018). Women leaders and firm performance in family businesses: An examination of financial and nonfinancial outcomes. *Journal of Family Business Strategy*, *9*(4), 238–49.

Chen, H.-L., & Hsu, W.-T. (2009). Family ownership, board independence, and R&D investment. *Family Business Review*, *22*(4), 347–62.

Chirico, F., Gómez-Mejia, L. R., Hellerstedt, K., Withers, M., & Nordqvist, M. (2020). To merge, sell, or liquidate? Socioemotional wealth, family control, and the choice of business exit. *Journal of Management*, *46* (8), 1342–79.

Chirico, F., & Salvato, C. (2016). Knowledge internalization and product development in family firms: When relational and affective factors matter. *Entrepreneurship Theory and Practice*, *40*(1), 201–29.

Chirico, F., Welsh, D. H., Ireland, R. D., & Sieger, P. (2021). Family versus non-family firm franchisors: Behavioural and performance differences. *Journal of Management Studies*, *58*(1), 165–200.

Chrisman, J. J., Chua, J. H., De Massis, A., Frattini, F., & Wright, M. (2015). The ability and willingness paradox in family firm innovation. *Journal of Product Innovation Management*, *32*(3), 310–18.

Chrisman, J. J., Chua, J. H., & Litz, R. (2003a). A unified systems perspective of family firm performance: An extension and integration. *Journal of Business Venturing*, *18*(4), 467–72.

Chrisman, J. J., Chua, J. H., Pearson, A. W., & Barnett, T. (2012). Family involvement, family influence, and family–centered non–economic goals in small firms. *Entrepreneurship Theory and Practice*, *36*(2), 267–93.

Chrisman, J. J., Chua, J. H., & Sharma, P. (2003b). Current trends and future directions in family business management studies: Toward a theory of the family firm. *Coleman white paper series*, *4*(1), 1–63.

Chrisman, J. J., Chua, J. H., & Sharma, P. (2005). Trends and directions in the development of a strategic management theory of the family firm. *Entrepreneurship Theory and Practice*, *29*(5), 555–75.

Chrisman, J. J., Madison, K., & Kim, T. (2021). A dynamic framework of noneconomic goals and inter-family agency complexities in multi-family firms. *Entrepreneurship Theory and Practice*, *45*(4), 906–30.

Chrisman, J. J., Memili, E., & Misra, K. (2014). Nonfamily managers, family firms, and the winner's curse: The influence of noneconomic goals and bounded rationality. *Entrepreneurship Theory and Practice*, *38*(5), 1–25.

Chrisman, J. J., & Patel, P. C. (2012). Variations in R&D investments of family and nonfamily firms: Behavioral agency and myopic loss aversion perspectives. *Academy of Management Journal*, *55*(4), 976–97.

Chua, J. H., Chrisman, J. J., & Sharma, P. (1999). Defining the family business by behavior. *Entrepreneurship Theory and Practice*, *23*(4), 19–39.

Chua, J. H., Chrisman, J. J., & Steier, L. P. (2003). Extending the theoretical horizons of family business research. *Entrepreneurship Theory and Practice*, *27*(4), 331–38.

Chua, J. H., Chrisman, J. J., Steier, L. P., & Rau, S. B. (2012). Sources of heterogeneity in family firms: An introduction.*Entrepreneurship Theory and Practice*, *36*(6), 1103–13.

Chung, C.-N., & Luo, X. (2008). Institutional logics or agency costs: The influence of corporate governance models on business group restructuring in emerging economies. *Organization Science*, *19*(5), 766–84.

Claessens, S., Djankov, S., & Lang, L. H. (2000). The separation of ownership and control in East Asian corporations. *Journal of Financial Economics*, *58* (1–2), 81–112.

Clinton, E., McAdam, M., & Gamble, J. R. (2018). Transgenerational entrepreneurial family firms: An examination of the business model construct. *Journal of Business Research*, *90*, 269–85.

Colli, A. (2012). Contextualizing performances of family firms: The perspective of business history. *Family Business Review*, *25*(3), 243–57.

Craig, J., & Dibrell, C. (2006). The natural environment, innovation, and firm performance: A comparative study. *Family Business Review*, *19*(4), 275–88.

Cruz, C., Justo, R., Larraza-Kintana, M., & Garcés-Galdeano, L. (2019). When do women make a better table? examining the influence of women directors on family firm's corporate social performance. *Entrepreneurship Theory and Practice*, *43*(2), 282–301.

Cruz, C., & Nordqvist, M. (2012). Entrepreneurial orientation in family firms: A generational perspective. *Small Business Economics*, *38*(1), 33–49.

Cruz, C. C., Gómez-Mejia, L. R., & Becerra, M. (2010). Perceptions of benevolence and the design of agency contracts: CEO-TMT relationships in family firms. *Academy of Management Journal*, *53*(1), 69–89.

Dacin, M. T., Dacin, P. A., & Kent, D. (2019). Tradition in organizations: A custodianship framework. *Academy of Management Annals*, *13*(1), 342–73.

Daily, C. M., & Dollinger, M. J. (1992). An empirical examination of ownership structure in family and professionally managed firms. *Family Business Review*, *5*(2), 117–36.

De Massis, A., Audretsch, D., Uhlaner, L., & Kammerlander, N. (2018a). Innovation with Limited Resources: Management Lessons from the German Mittelstand. *Journal of Product Innovation Management*, *35*(1), 125–46.

De Massis, A., Audretsch, D., Uhlaner, L., & Kammerlander, N. (2018b). Innovation with limited resources: Management lessons from the German Mittelstand. *Journal of Product Innovation Management*, *35* (1), 125–46.

De Massis, A., Chirico, F., Kotlar, J., & Naldi, L. (2014). The temporal evolution of proactiveness in family firms: The horizontal S-curve hypothesis. *Family Business Review*, *27*(1), 35–50.

De Massis, A., Chua, J. H., & Chrisman, J. J. (2008). Factors preventing intra-family succession. *Family Business Review, 21*(2), 183–99.

De Massis, A., Eddleston, K. A., & Rovelli, P. (2021). Entrepreneurial by design: How organizational design affects family and nonfamily firms' opportunity exploitation. *Journal of Management Studies, 58*(1), 27–62.

De Massis, A., & Foss, N. J. (2018). Advancing family business research: The promise of microfoundations.*Family Business Review, 31*(4), 386–96.

De Massis, A., Frattini, F., Kotlar, J., Petruzzelli, A. M., & Wright, M. (2016). Innovation through tradition: Lessons from innovative family businesses and directions for future research. *Academy of Management Perspectives, 30*(1), 93–116.

De Massis, A., Frattini, F., Pizzurno, E., & Cassia, L. (2015). Product innovation in family versus nonfamily firms: An exploratory analysis. *Journal of Small Business Management, 53*(1), 1–36.

De Massis, A., Kotlar, J., & Campopiano, G. (2013). Dispersion of family ownership and the performance of small-to-medium size private family firms. *Journal of Family Business Strategy, 4*(3), 166–75.

Debicki, B. J., Kellermanns, F. W., Chrisman, J. J., Pearson, A. W., & Spencer, B. A. (2016). Development of a socioemotional wealth importance (SEWi) scale for family firm research. *Journal of Family Business Strategy, 7*(1), 47–57.

Debicki, B. J., Matherne III, C. F., Kellermanns, F. W., & Chrisman, J. J. (2009). Family business research in the new millennium: An overview of the who, the where, the what, and the why. *Family Business Review, 22*(2), 151–66.

Deephouse, D. L. (1999). To be different, or to be the same? It's a question (and theory) of strategic balance. *Strategic Management Journal, 20*(2), 147–66.

Deephouse, D. L., & Jaskiewicz, P. (2013). Do family firms have better reputations than non-family firms? An integration of socioemotional wealth and social identity theories. *Journal of Management Studies, 50*(3), 337–60.

Diaz-Moriana, V., Clinton, E., Kammerlander, N., Lumpkin, G., & Craig, J. B. (2020). Innovation motives in family firms: A transgenerational view. *Entrepreneurship Theory and Practice, 44*(2), 256–87.

Diéguez-Soto, J., Manzaneque, M., & Rojo-Ramírez, A. A. (2016). Technological innovation inputs, outputs, and performance: The moderating role of family involvement in management. *Family Business Review, 29*(3), 327–46.

Dieleman, M., & Koning, J. (2019). Articulating values through identity work: Advancing family business ethics research. *Journal of Business Ethics, 163*, 675–87.

Dodd, S. D., Anderson, A., & Jack, S. (2013). Being in time and the family owned firm. *Scandinavian Journal of Management, 29*(1), 35–47.

Doherty, B., Haugh, H., & Lyon, F. (2014). Social enterprises as hybrid organizations: A review and research agenda. *International Journal of Management Reviews, 16*(4), 417–36.

Dunn, B. (1995). Success themes in Scottish family enterprises: Philosophies and practices through the generations. *Family Business Review, 8*(1), 17–28.

Duran, P., Kammerlander, N., Van Essen, M., & Zellweger, T. (2016). Doing more with less: Innovation input and output in family firms. *Academy of Management Journal, 59*(4), 1224–64.

Dyer Jr, W. G., & Whetten, D. A. (2006). Family firms and social responsibility: Preliminary evidence from the S&P 500. *Entrepreneurship Theory and Practice, 30*(6), 785–802.

Eddleston, K. A., Banalieva, E. R., & Verbeke, A. (2020). The bribery paradox in transition economies and the enactment of 'new normal' business environments. *Journal of Management Studies, 57*(3), 597–625.

Eddleston, K. A., Otondo, R. F., & Kellermanns, F. W. (2008). Conflict, participative decision-making, and generational ownership dispersion: A multilevel analysis. *Journal of Small Business Management, 46*(3), 456–83.

Erdogan, I., Rondi, E., & De Massis, A. (2020). Managing the tradition and innovation paradox in family firms: A family imprinting perspective. *Entrepreneurship Theory and Practice, 44*(1), 20–54.

Faccio, M., & Lang, L. H. (2002). The ultimate ownership of Western European corporations. *Journal of Financial Economics, 65*(3), 365–95.

Fahed-Sreih, J., & Djoundourian, S. (2006). Determinants of longevity and success in Lebanese family businesses: An exploratory study. *Family Business Review, 19*(3), 225–34.

Fairclough, S., & Micelotta, E. R. (2013). Beyond the family firm: Reasserting the influence of the family institutional logic across organizations. In M. Lounsbury & E. Boxenbaum (Eds.) *Institutional logics in action, part B* (pp. 63–98). Emerald Group.

Feldman, E. R., Amit, R., & Villalonga, B. (2016). Corporate divestitures and family control. *Strategic Management Journal, 37*(3), 429–46.

Fletcher, D., De Massis, A., & Nordqvist, M. (2016). Qualitative research practices and family business scholarship: A review and future research agenda. *Journal of Family Business Strategy, 7*(1), 8–25.

Friedland, R., & Alford, R. R. (1991). Bringing society back in: Symbols, practices, and institutional contradictions. In W. W. Powell & P. J. DiMaggio

(Eds.), *The new institutionalism in organizational analysis* (pp. 232–63). University of Chicago Press.

Fuetsch, E., & Suess-Reyes, J. (2017). Research on innovation in family businesses: Are we building an ivory tower? *Journal of Family Business Management, 7*(1), 44–92.

García-Álvarez, E., & López-Sintas, J. (2001). A taxonomy of founders based on values: The root of family business heterogeneity. *Family Business Review, 14*(3), 209–30.

García-Ramos, R., & García-Olalla, M. (2011). Board characteristics and firm performance in public founder-and nonfounder-led family businesses. *Journal of Family Business Strategy, 2*(4), 220–31.

Ge, B., De Massis, A., & Kotlar, J. (2022). Mining the past: History scripting strategies and competitive advantage in a family business. *Entrepreneurship Theory and Practice, 46*(1), 223–51.

Ge, J., & Micelotta, E. (2019). When does the family matter? Institutional pressures and corporate philanthropy in China. *Organization Studies, 40*(6), 833–57.

Gedajlovic, E., Carney, M., Chrisman, J. J., & Kellermanns, F. W. (2012). The adolescence of family firm research: Taking stock and planning for the future. *Journal of Management, 38*(4), 1010–37.

Geeraerts, G. (1984). The effect of ownership on the organization structure in small firms. *Administrative Science Quarterly, 29*(2), 232–37.

Gereffi, G., Humphrey, J., & Sturgeon, T. (2005). The governance of global value chains. *Review of International Political Economy, 12*(1), 78–104.

Gilding, M., Gregory, S., & Cosson, B. (2015). Motives and outcomes in family business succession planning. *Entrepreneurship Theory and Practice, 39*(2), 299–312.

Gioia, D. A., Price, K. N., Hamilton, A. L., & Thomas, J. B. (2010). Forging an identity: An insider-outsider study of processes involved in the formation of organizational identity. *Administrative Science Quarterly, 55*(1), 1–46.

Glynn, M. A. (2000). When cymbals become symbols: Conflict over organizational identity within a symphony orchestra. *Organization Science, 11*(3), 285–98.

Goel, S., & Jones III, R. J. (2016). Entrepreneurial exploration and exploitation in family business: A systematic review and future directions. *Family Business Review, 29*(1), 94–120.

Gomez-Mejia, L. R., Cruz, C., Berrone, P., & De Castro, J. (2011). The bind that ties: Socioemotional wealth preservation in family firms. *Academy of Management Annals, 5*(1), 653–707.

Gomez-Mejia, L. R., Haynes, K. T., Núñez-Nickel, M., Jacobson, K. J., & Moyano-Fuentes, J. (2007). Socioemotional wealth and business risks in family-controlled firms: Evidence from Spanish olive oil mills. *Administrative Science Quarterly*, *52*(1), 106–37.

Gomez-Mejia, L. R., Nuñez -Nickel, M., & Gutierrez, I. (2001). The role of family ties in agency contracts. *Academy of Management Journal*, *44*(1), 81–95.

Gomez-Mejia, L. R., Patel, P. C., & Zellweger, T. M. (2018). In the horns of the dilemma: Socioemotional wealth, financial wealth, and acquisitions in family firms. *Journal of Management*, *44*(4), 1369–97.

Gotsi, M., Andriopoulos, C., Lewis, M. W., & Ingram, A. E. (2010). Managing creatives: Paradoxical approaches to identity regulation. *Human Relations*, *63*(6), 781–805.

Granqvist, N., & Gustafsson, R. (2016). Temporal institutional work. *Academy of Management Journal*, *59*(3), 1009–35.

Greenwood, R., Cooper, D. J., Hinings, C., & Brown, J. L. (1993). Biggest is best? Strategic assumptions and actions in the Canadian audit industry. *Canadian Journal of Administrative Sciences/Revue Canadienne des Sciences de l'Administration*, *10*(4), 308–21.

Greenwood, R., Raynard, M., Kodeih, F., Micelotta, E. R., & Lounsbury, M. (2011). Institutional complexity and organizational responses. *Academy of Management Annals*, *5*(1), 317–71.

Greenwood, R., & Suddaby, R. (2006). Institutional entrepreneurship in mature fields: The big five accounting firms. *Academy of Management Journal*, *49*(1), 27–48.

Habbershon, T. G., Nordqvist, M., & Zellweger, T. (2010). Transgenerational entrepreneurship. In M. Nordqvist & T. Zellweger (Eds.), *Transgenerational entrepreneurship: Exploring growth and performance in family firms across generations* (pp. 1–38). Edward Elgar.

Habbershon, T. G., & Pistrui, J. (2002). Enterprising families domain: Family-influenced ownership groups in pursuit of transgenerational wealth. *Family Business Review*, *15*(3), 223–37.

Habbershon, T. G., & Williams, M. L. (1999). A resource-based framework for assessing the strategic advantages of family firms. *Family Business Review*, *12*(1), 1–25.

Hannan, M. T., Pólos, L., & Carroll, G. R. (2007). Language Matters, from *Logics of Organization Theory: Audiences, Codes, and Ecologies*. Introductory Chapters. In Logics of Organization Theory: Audiences, Codes, and Ecologies. Princeton University Press.

Harveston, P. D., Davis, P. S., & Lyden, J. A. (1997). Succession planning in family business. The impact of owner gender. *Family Business Review*, *10*(4), 373–96.

Hauck, J., Suess-Reyes, J., Beck, S., Prügl, R., & Frank, H. (2016). Measuring socioemotional wealth in family-owned and-managed firms: A validation and short form of the FIBER Scale. *Journal of Family Business Strategy*, *7*(3), 133–48.

Heck, R. K., & Stafford, K. (2001). The vital institution of family business: Economic benefits hidden in plain sight. *Destroying Myths and Creating Value in Family Business*, 9–17.

Hiebl, M. R. (2015). Family involvement and organizational ambidexterity in later-generation family businesses: A framework for further investigation. *Management Decision*, *53*(5), 1061–82.

Hinings, B., & Meyer, R. E. (2018). *Starting points: Intellectual and institutional foundations of organization theory*. Cambridge University Press.

Hjorth, D., & Dawson, A. (2016). The burden of history in the family business organization. *Organization Studies*, *37*(8), 1089–111.

Hoffman, J., Hoelscher, M., & Sorenson, R. (2006). Achieving sustained competitive advantage: A family capital theory. *Family Business Review*, *19*(2), 135–45.

Holt, D. T., Pearson, A. W., Payne, G. T., & Sharma, P. (2018). Family business research as a boundary-spanning platform. *Family Business Review*, *31*(1), 14–31.

Hoy, F., & Sharma, P. (2006). Navigating the family business education maze. *Handbook of Research on Family Business*, *49*, 11–24.

Huang, R. H., & Orr, G. (2007). China's state-owned enterprises: Board governance and the Communist Party. *McKinsey Quarterly*, *1*, 108.

Huang, X., Chen, L., Xu, E., Lu, F., & Tam, K. C. (2020). Shadow of the prince: Parent-incumbents' coercive control over child-successors in family organizations. *Administrative Science Quarterly*, *65*(3), 719–50.

Huff, A. S. (1999). *Writing for scholarly publication*. Sage.

Ingram, A. E., Lewis, M. W., Barton, S., & Gartner, W. B. (2016). Paradoxes and innovation in family firms: The role of paradoxical thinking. *Entrepreneurship Theory and Practice*, *40*(1), 161–76.

James, A. E., Jennings, J. E., & Breitkreuz, R. S. (2012). Worlds apart? Rebridging the distance between family science and family business research. *Family Business Review*, *25*(1), 87–108.

Jansen, J. J., Tempelaar, M. P., Van den Bosch, F. A., & Volberda, H. W. (2009). Structural differentiation and ambidexterity: The mediating role of integration mechanisms. *Organization Science*, *20*(4), 797–811.

Jaskiewicz, P., Block, J. H., Miller, D., & Combs, J. G. (2017a). Founder versus family owners' impact on pay dispersion among non-CEO top managers: Implications for firm performance. *Journal of Management*, *43* (5), 1524–52.

Jaskiewicz, P., Combs, J. G., & Rau, S. B. (2015). Entrepreneurial legacy: Toward a theory of how some family firms nurture transgenerational entrepreneurship. *Journal of Business Venturing, 30*(1), 29–49.

Jaskiewicz, P., Combs, J. G., Shanine, K. K., & Kacmar, K. M. (2017b). Introducing the family: A review of family science with implications for management research. *Academy of Management Annals, 11*(1), 309–41.

Jaskiewicz, P., Heinrichs, K., Rau, S. B., & Reay, T. (2016). To be or not to be: How family firms manage family and commercial logics in succession. *Entrepreneurship Theory and Practice, 40*(4), 781–813.

Jaskiewicz, P., & Luchak, A. A. (2013). Explaining performance differences between family firms with family and nonfamily CEOs: It's the nature of the tie to the family that counts! *Entrepreneurship Theory and Practice, 37*(6), 1361–67.

Jaskiewicz, P., Neubaum, D. O., De Massis, A., & Holt, D. T. (2020). The adulthood of family business research through inbound and outbound theorizing. *Family Business Review, 33*(1), 10–17.

Jaskiewicz, P., & Rau, S. B. (2021). *Enabling next generation legacies: 35 questions that next generation members in enterprising families ask.* Family Enterprise Knowledge Hub Publishing.

Jay, J. (2013). Navigating paradox as a mechanism of change and innovation in hybrid organizations. *Academy of Management Journal, 56*(1), 137–59.

Jiang, D. S., Kellermanns, F. W., Munyon, T. P., & Morris, M. L. (2018). More than meets the eye: A review and future directions for the social psychology of socioemotional wealth. *Family Business Review, 31*(1), 125–57.

Kammerlander, N., Dessi, C., Bird, M., Floris, M., & Murru, A. (2015). The impact of shared stories on family firm innovation: A multicase study. *Family Business Review, 28*(4), 332–54.

Kammerlander, N., Patzelt, H., Behrens, J., & Röhm, C. (2020). Organizational ambidexterity in family-managed firms: The role of family involvement in top management. *Family Business Review, 33*(4), 393–423.

Kammerlander, N., & van Essen, M. (2017). Family firms are more innovative than other companies. *Harvard Business Review.* Available at https://hbr.org/2017/01/research-family-firms-are-more-innovative-than-other-companies (Accessed March 29, 2017)

Kaplan, S., & Orlikowski, W. J. (2013). Temporal work in strategy making. *Organization Science, 24*(4), 965–95.

Kellermanns, F. W., & Eddleston, K. A. (2006). Corporate entrepreneurship in family firms: A family perspective. *Entrepreneurship Theory and Practice, 30*(6), 809–30.

Kellermanns, F. W., Eddleston, K. A., Barnett, T., & Pearson, A. (2008). An exploratory study of family member characteristics and involvement: Effects on entrepreneurial behavior in the family firm. *Family Business Review, 21* (1), 1–14.

King, B. G., & Whetten, D. A. (2008). Rethinking the relationship between reputation and legitimacy: A social actor conceptualization. *Corporate Reputation Review, 11*(3), 192–207.

Klein, S. B., Astrachan, J. H., & Smyrnios, K. X. (2005). The F–PEC scale of family influence: Construction, validation, and further implication for theory. *Entrepreneurship Theory and Practice, 29*(3), 321–39.

Kohli, M., & Künemund, H. (2003). Der Alters-Survey: Die zweite Lebenshälfte im Spiegel repräsentativer Daten. *Aus Politik und Zeitgeschichte, 20*(2003), 18–25.

König, A., Kammerlander, N., & Enders, A. (2013). The family innovator's dilemma: How family influence affects the adoption of discontinuous technologies by incumbent firms. *Academy of Management Review, 38*(3), 418–41.

Kotlar, J., & De Massis, A. (2013). Goal setting in family firms: Goal diversity, social interactions, and collective commitment to family–centered goals. *Entrepreneurship Theory and Practice, 37*(6), 1263–88.

Kraatz, M. S., & Block, E. S. (2008). Organizational implications of institutional pluralism. *The SAGE Handbook of Organizational Institutionalism, 840*, 243–75.

Kroeze, R., & Keulen, S. (2013). Leading a multinational is history in practice: The use of invented traditions and narratives at AkzoNobel, Shell, Philips and ABN AMRO. *Business History, 55*(8), 1265–87.

Kroezen, J., Ravasi, D., Sasaki, I., Żebrowska, M., & Suddaby, R. (2021). Configurations of craft: Alternative models for organizing work. *Academy of Management Annals, 15*(2), 502–36.

Kunisch, S., Bartunek, J. M., Mueller, J., & Huy, Q. N. (2017). Time in strategic change research. *Academy of Management Annals, 11*(2), 1005–64.

La Porta, R., Lopez-de-Silanes, F., & Shleifer, A. (1999). Corporate ownership around the world. *The Journal of Finance, 54*(2), 471–517.

LaChapelle, K., & Barnes, L. B. (1998). The trust catalyst in family-owned businesses. *Family Business Review, 11*(1), 1–17.

Langley, A. N. N., Smallman, C., Tsoukas, H., & Van de Ven, A. H. (2013). Process studies of change in organization and management: Unveiling temporality, activity, and flow. *Academy of Management Journal, 56*(1), 1–13.

Lavie, D., Stettner, U., & Tushman, M. L. (2010). Exploration and exploitation within and across organizations. *Academy of Management Annals, 4* (1), 109–55.

Lawrence, P. R., & Lorsch, J. W. (1967). Differentiation and integration in complex organizations. *Administrative Science Quarterly, 12*(1), 1–47.

Lawrence, T. B., Winn, M. I., & Jennings, P. D. (2001). The temporal dynamics of institutionalization. *Academy of Management Review, 26*(4), 624–44.

Le Breton-Miller, I., & Miller, D. (2018). Looking back at and forward from: "Family governance and firm performance: Agency, stewardship, and capabilities." *Family Business Review, 31*(2), 229–37.

Le Breton–Miller, I., & Miller, D. (2006). Why do some family businesses out–compete? Governance, long–term orientations, and sustainable capability. *Entrepreneurship Theory and Practice, 30*(6), 731–46.

Le Breton-Miller, I., Miller, D., & Lester, R. H. (2011). Stewardship or agency? A social embeddedness reconciliation of conduct and performance in public family businesses. *Organization Science, 22*(3), 704–21.

Le Breton–Miller, I., Miller, D., & Steier, L. P. (2004). Toward an integrative model of effective FOB succession. *Entrepreneurship Theory and Practice, 28*(4), 305–28.

Leaptrott, J. (2005). An institutional theory view of the family business. *Family Business Review, 18*(3), 215–28.

Lee, K. S., Lim, G. H., & Lim, W. S. (2003). Family business succession: Appropriation risk and choice of successor. *Academy of Management Review, 28*(4), 657–66.

Leitterstorf, M. P., & Rau, S. B. (2014). Socioemotional wealth and IPO underpricing of family firms. *Strategic Management Journal, 35*(5), 751–60.

Lewis, M. W. (2000). Exploring paradox: Toward a more comprehensive guide. *Academy of Management Review, 25*(4), 760–76.

Li, J. B., & Piezunka, H. (2020). The uniplex third: Enabling single-domain role transitions in multiplex relationships. *Administrative Science Quarterly, 65*(2), 314–58.

Ling, Y., & Kellermanns, F. W. (2010). The effects of family firm specific sources of TMT diversity: The moderating role of information exchange frequency. *Journal of Management Studies, 47*(2), 322–44.

Lingo, E. L., & Elmes, M. B. (2019). Institutional preservation work at a family business in crisis: Micro-processes, emotions, and nonfamily members. *Organization Studies, 40*(6), 887–916.

Litz, R. A. (2008). Two sides of a one-sided phenomenon: conceptualizing the family business and business family as a möbius strip. *Family Business Review, 21*(3), 217–36.

Lumpkin, G. T., Brigham, K. H., & Moss, T. W. (2010). Long-term orientation: Implications for the entrepreneurial orientation and performance of family businesses. *Entrepreneurship & Regional Development, 22*(3–4), 241–64.

Luo, X. R., Jeong, Y.-C., & Chung, C.-N. (2019). In the eye of the beholder: Global analysts' coverage of family firms in an emerging market. *Journal of Management*, *45*(5), 1830–57.

Magrelli, V., Rondi, E., De Massis, A., & Kotlar, J. (2022a). Generational brokerage: An intersubjective perspective on managing temporal orientations in family firm succession. *Strategic Organization*, *20*(1), 164–99.

Magrelli, V., Rovelli, P., Benedetti, C., Überbacher, R., & De Massis, A. (2022b). Generations in family business: a multifield review and future research agenda. *Family Business Review*, *35*(1), 15–44.

Mahto, R. V., Davis, P. S., & Khanin, D. (2013). Continuation commitment: Family's commitment to continue the family business. *Journal of Family and Economic Issues*, *35*(2), 1–12.

Mair, J., Battilana, J., & Cardenas, J. (2012). Organizing for society: A typology of social entrepreneuring models. *Journal of Business Ethics*, *111*(3), 353–73.

Marquis, C., & Lounsbury, M. (2007). Vive la résistance: Competing logics and the consolidation of US community banking. *Academy of Management Journal*, *50*(4), 799–820.

McAdam, M., Clinton, E., & Dibrell, C. (2020). Navigation of the paradoxical landscape of the family business. *International Small Business Journal*, *38* (3), 139–53.

McKenny, A. F., Short, J. C., Zachary, M. A., & Payne, G. T. (2012). Assessing espoused goals in private family firms using content analysis. *Family Business Review*, *25*(3), 298–317.

Melin, L., & Nordqvist, M. (2007). The reflexive dynamics of institutional-ization: The case of the family business. *Strategic Organization*, *5*(3), 321–33.

Meyer, J. (2019). Outreach and performance of microfinance institutions: The importance of portfolio yield. *Applied Economics*, *51*(27), 2945–62.

Micelotta, E., Glaser, V. L., & Dorian, G. (2020). Qualitative research in family business: methodological insights to leverage inspiration, avoid data asphyxiation and develop robust theory. In A. De Massis and N. Kammerlander (Eds.). *Handbook of Qualitative Research Methods for Family Business* (pp. 25–47). Edward Elgar.

Miller, D., Amore, M. D., Le Breton-Miller, I., Minichilli, A., & Quarato, F. (2018). Strategic distinctiveness in family firms: Firm institutional hetero-geneity and configurational multidimensionality. *Journal of Family Business Strategy*, *9*(1), 16–26.

Miller, D., & Le Breton-Miller, I. (2005). *Managing for the long run: Lessons in competitive advantage from great family businesses*. Harvard Business Press.

Miller, D., & Le Breton-Miller, I. (2006). The best of both worlds: Exploitation and exploration in successful family businesses. In J. A. C. Baum, S. D. Dobrev, & A. Van Witteloostuijn (Eds.), *Ecology and Strategy* (pp. 215–40). Emerald Group.

Miller, D., Le Breton-Miller, I., Amore, M. D., Minichilli, A., & Corbetta, G. (2017). Institutional logics, family firm governance and performance. *Journal of Business Venturing, 32*(6), 674–93.

Miller, D., Le Breton-Miller, I., & Lester, R. H. (2011). Family and lone founder ownership and strategic behaviour: Social context, identity, and institutional logics. *Journal of Management Studies, 48*(1), 1–25.

Miller, D., Minichilli, A., & Corbetta, G. (2013). Is family leadership always beneficial? *Strategic Management Journal, 34*(5), 553–71.

Minichilli, A., Corbetta, G., & MacMillan, I. C. (2010a). Top management teams in family-controlled companies: "Familiness," "faultlines," and their impact on financial performance. *Journal of Management Studies, 47*(2), 205–22.

Minichilli, A., Nordqvist, M., Corbetta, G., & Amore, M. D. (2014). CEO succession mechanisms, organizational context, and performance: A socio-emotional wealth perspective on family-controlled firms. *Journal of Management Studies, 51*(7), 1153–79.

Minkoff, D. C. (2002). The emergence of hybrid organizational forms: Combining identity-based service provision and political action. *Nonprofit and Voluntary Sector Quarterly, 31*(3), 377–401.

Minola, T., Kammerlander, N., Kellermanns, F. W., & Hoy, F. (2021). Corporate entrepreneurship and family business: Learning across domains. *Journal of Management Studies, 58*(1), 1–26.

Molly, V., Laveren, E., & Deloof, M. (2010). Family business succession and its impact on financial structure and performance. *Family Business Review, 23*(2), 131–47.

Moores, K. (2009). Paradigms and theory building in the domain of business families. *Family Business Review, 22*(2), 167–80.

Morris, M. H. (1998). *Entrepreneurial intensity.* Quorum Books.

Mosakowski, E., & Earley, P. C. (2000). A selective review of time assumptions in strategy research. *Academy of Management Review, 25*(4), 796–812.

Moss, T. W., Payne, G. T., & Moore, C. B. (2014). Strategic consistency of exploration and exploitation in family businesses. *Family Business Review, 27*(1), 51–71.

Moss, T. W., Short, J. C., Payne, G. T., & Lumpkin, G. (2011). Dual identities in social ventures: An exploratory study. *Entrepreneurship Theory and Practice, 35*(4), 805–30.

Murray, F. (2010). The oncomouse that roared: Hybrid exchange strategies as a source of distinction at the boundary of overlapping institutions. *American Journal of Sociology, 116*(2), 341–88.

Muzio, D., Aulakh, S., & Kirkpatrick, I. (2019). *Professional occupations and organizations.* Cambridge UniversityPress.

Naldi, L., Cennamo, C., Corbetta, G., & Gomez–Mejia, L. (2013). Preserving socioemotional wealth in family firms: Asset or liability? The moderating role of business context. *Entrepreneurship, Theory and Practice, 37*(6), 1341–60.

Nason, R., Mazzelli, A., & Carney, M. (2019). The ties that unbind: Socialization and business-owning family reference point shift. *Academy of Management Review, 44*(4), 846–70.

Neubaum, D. O., & Micelotta, E. (2021). WANTED—Theoretical contributions: An editorial on the pitfalls and pathways in family business research. *Family Business Review, 34*(3), 242–50.

Nordqvist, M., & Zellweger, T. (2010). *Transgenerational entrepreneurship: Exploring growth and performance in family firms across generations.* Edward Elgar.

Odom, D. L., Chang, E. P., Chrisman, J. J., Sharma, P., & Steier, L. (2019). The most influential family business articles from 2006 to 2013 using five theoretical perspectives. In E. Memili & C. Dibrell (Eds.). *The Palgrave handbook of heterogeneity among family firms* (pp. 41–67). Palgrave Macmillan.

O'Reilly III C. A., & Tushman, M. L. (2013). Organizational ambidexterity: Past, present, and future. *Academy of Management Perspectives, 27*(4), 324–38.

Özsomer, A., Calantone, R. J., & Di Bonetto, A. (1997). What makes firms more innovative? A look at organizational and environmental factors. *Journal of Business & Industrial Marketing, 12*(6), 400–16.

Pache, A.-C., & Santos, F. (2013). Inside the hybrid organization: Selective coupling as a response to competing institutional logics. *Academy of Management Journal, 56*(4), 972–1001.

Patel, P. C., & Cooper, D. (2014). Structural power equality between family and non-family TMT members and the performance of family firms. *Academy of Management Journal, 57*(6), 1624–49.

Payne, G. T. (2018). Reflections on family business research: Considering domains and theory. *Family Business Review, 31*(2), 167–75.

Petriglieri, G., & Stein, M. (2012). The unwanted self: Projective identification in leaders' identity work. *Organization Studies, 33*(9), 1217–35.

Pieper, T. M., & Klein, S. B. (2007). The bulleye: A systems approach to modeling family firms. *Family Business Review, 20*(4), 301–19.

Podolny, J. M., & Page, K. L. (1998). Network forms of organization. *Annual Review of Sociology, 24*(1), 57–76.

Ponroy, J. V., Lê, P., & Pradies, C. (2019). In a family way? A model of family firm identity maintenance by non-family members. *Organization Studies, 40* (6), 859–86.

Poole, M. S., & Van de Ven, A. H. (1989). Using paradox to build management and organization theories. *Academy of Management Review, 14*(4), 562–78.

Porfírio, J. A., Felício, J. A., & Carrilho, T. (2020). Family business succession: Analysis of the drivers of success based on entrepreneurship theory. *Journal of Business Research, 115*, 250–57.

Powell, G. N., & Eddleston, K. A. (2017). Family involvement in the firm, family-to-business support, and entrepreneurial outcomes: An exploration. *Journal of Small Business Management, 55*(4), 614–31.

Powell, W. W., & Sandholtz, K. W. (2012). Amphibious entrepreneurs and the emergence of organizational forms. *Strategic Entrepreneurship Journal, 6* (2), 94–115.

Pratt, M. G., & Rafaeli, A. (1997). Organizational dress as a symbol of multi-layered social identities. *Academy of Management Journal, 40*(4), 862–98.

Prügl, R., & Spitzley, D. I. (2021). Responding to digital transformation by external corporate venturing: An enterprising family identity and communication patterns perspective. *Journal of Management Studies, 58*(1), 135–64.

Radu-Lefebvre, M., & Randerson, K. (2020). Successfully navigating the paradox of control and autonomy in succession: The role of managing ambivalent emotions. *International Small Business Journal, 38*(3), 184–210.

Raffaelli, R. (2019). Technology reemergence: Creating new value for old technologies in Swiss mechanical watchmaking, 1970–2008. *Administrative Science Quarterly, 64*(3), 576–618.

Raffaelli, R., DeJordy, R., & McDonald, R. M. (2021). How leaders with divergent visions generate novel strategy: Navigating the paradox of preservation and modernization in Swiss watchmaking. *Academy of Management Journal, 65*(5), 1593–1622.

Raisch, S., & Birkinshaw, J. (2008). Organizational ambidexterity: Antecedents, outcomes, and moderators. *Journal of Management, 34*(3), 375–409.

Raitis, J., Sasaki, I., & Kotlar, J. (2021). System-spanning values work and entrepreneurial growth in family firms. *Journal of Management Studies, 58* (1), 104–34.

Ramírez-Pasillas, M., Lundberg, H., & Nordqvist, M. (2021). Next generation external venturing practices in family owned businesses. *Journal of Management Studies, 58*(1), 63–103.

Reay, T., Goodrick, E., & D'Aunno, T. (2021). *Health care research and organization theory.* Cambridge University Press.

Reay, T., Jaskiewicz, P., & Hinings, C. (2015). How family, business, and community logics shape family firm behavior and "rules of the game" in an organizational field. *Family Business Review, 28*(4), 292–311.

Reay, T., & Whetten, D. A. (2011). What constitutes a theoretical contribution in family business?. *Family Business Review, 24*(2), 105–10.

Reay, T., Zilber, T. B., Langley, A., & Tsoukas, H. (2019). *Institutions and organizations: A process view.* Oxford University Press.

Reinecke, J., & Lawrence, T. B. (in press). The role of temporality in institutional stabilization: A process view. *Academy of Management Review.*

Reinecke, J., Suddaby, R., Tsoukas, H., & Langley, A. (2021). *Time, temporality, and history in process organization studies.* Oxford University Press.

Richards, M., Zellweger, T., & Gond, J. P. (2017). Maintaining moral legitimacy through worlds and words: an explanation of firms' investment in sustainability certification. *Journal of Management Studies, 54*(5), 676–710.

Rocha, H. O., & Ghoshal, S. (2006). Beyond self-interest revisited. *Journal of Management Studies, 43*(3), 585–619.

Röd, I. (2016). Disentangling the family firm's innovation process: A systematic review. *Journal of Family Business Strategy, 7*(3), 185–201.

Rondi, E., De Massis, A., & Kotlar, J. (2019). Unlocking innovation potential: A typology of family business innovation postures and the critical role of the family system. *Journal of Family Business Strategy, 10*(4), 100236.

Rousseau, D. M., & Fried, Y. (2001). Location, location, location: Contextualizing organizational research. *Journal of Organizational Behavior, 22*(1), 1–13.

Rovelli, P., Ferasso, M., De Massis, A., & Kraus, S. (2021). Thirty years of research in family business journals: Status quo and future directions. *Journal of Family Business Strategy, 13*(3), 1–17.

Ruef, M. (2000). The emergence of organizational forms: A community ecology approach. *American Journal of Sociology, 106*(3), 658–714.

Ruef, M., & Patterson, K. (2009). Credit and classification: The impact of industry boundaries in nineteenth-century America. *Administrative Science Quarterly, 54*(3), 486–520.

Salvato, C., Chirico, F., Melin, L., & Seidl, D. (2019). Coupling family business research with organization studies: Interpretations, issues and insights. *Organization Studies, 40*(6), 775–791.

Sasaki, I., Kotlar, J., Ravasi, D., & Vaara, E. (2020). Dealing with revered past: Historical identity statements and strategic change in Japanese family firms. *Strategic Management Journal, 41*(3), 590–623.

Sasaki, I., Ravasi, D., & Micelotta, E. (2019). Family firms as institutions: Cultural reproduction and status maintenance among multi-centenary shinise in Kyoto. *Organization Studies*, *40*(6), 793–831.

Schulze, W. S., & Gedajlovic, E. R. (2010). Whither family business? *Journal of Management Studies*, *47*(2), 191–204.

Schulze, W. S., Lubatkin, M. H., Dino, R. N., & Buchholtz, A. K. (2001). Agency relationships in family firms: Theory and evidence. *Organization Science*, *12*(2), 99–116.

Sciascia, S., & Mazzola, P. (2008). Family involvement in ownership and management: Exploring nonlinear effects on performance. *Family Business Review*, *21*(4), 331–45.

Sciascia, S., Mazzola, P., & Chirico, F. (2012). Generational involvement in the top management team of family firms: Exploring nonlinear effects on entrepreneurial orientation. *Entrepreneurship Theory and Practice*, *37*(1), 69–85.

Shane, S. A. (1996). Hybrid organizational arrangements and their implications for firm growth and survival: A study of new franchisors. *Academy of Management Journal*, *39*(1), 216–34.

Shanker, M. C., & Astrachan, J. H. (1996). Myths and realities: Family businesses' contribution to the US economy—A framework for assessing family business statistics. *Family Business Review*, *9*(2), 107–23.

Sharma, G., & Bansal, P. (2017). Partners for good: How business and NGOs engage the commercial–social paradox. *Organization Studies*, *38*(3–4), 341–64.

Sharma, P. (2004). An overview of the field of family business studies: Current status and directions for the future. *Family Business Review*, *17* (1), 1–36.

Sharma, P., Chrisman, J. J., & Gersick, K. E. (2012). 25 years of family business review: Reflections on the past and perspectives for the future. *Family Business Review*, *25*(1), 5–15.

Sharma, P., & Nordqvist, M. (2007). A typology for capturing the heterogeneity of family firms. In *Academy of Management Proceedings* (Vol. 2007, pp. 1–6). Academy of Management.

Sharma, P., & Nordqvist, M. (2008). A classification scheme for family firms: From family values to effective governance to firm performance. In J. Tàpies & J. L. Ward (Eds.), *Family Values and Value Creation* (pp. 71–101). Palgrave Macmillan.

Sharma, P., & Salvato, C. (2013). A balancing act between continuity and change. In P. F. Pérez & A. Colli (Eds.), *The Endurance of Family Businesses: A Global Overview* (pp. 34–56). Cambridge University Press.

Sharma, P., Salvato, C., & Reay, T. (2014). Temporal dimensions of family enterprise research. *Family Business Review, 27*(1), 10–19.

Shepherd, D., & Haynie, J. M. (2009). Family business, identity conflict, and an expedited entrepreneurial process: A process of resolving identity conflict. *Entrepreneurship Theory and Practice, 33*(6), 1245–64.

Simsek, Z. (2009). Organizational ambidexterity: Towards a multilevel understanding. *Journal of Management Studies, 46*(4), 597–624.

Sinha, P. N., Jaskiewicz, P., Gibb, J., & Combs, J. G. (2020). Managing history: How New Zealand's Gallagher Group used rhetorical narratives to reprioritize and modify imprinted strategic guideposts. *Strategic Management Journal, 41*(3), 557–89.

Smith, W. K., Erez, M., Jarvenpaa, S., Lewis, M. W., & Tracey, P. (2017). Adding complexity to theories of paradox, tensions, and dualities of innovation and change: Introduction to organization studies special issue on paradox, tensions, and dualities of innovation and change. *Organization Studies, 38*(3–4), 303–17.

Smith, W. K., & Lewis, M. W. (2011). Toward a theory of paradox: A dynamic equilibrium model of organizing. *Academy of Management Review, 36*(2), 381–403.

Smith, W. K., & Lewis, M. W. (2022). *Both/and thinking: Embracing creative tensions to solve your toughest problems.* Harvard Business Review Press.

Smith, W. K., & Tushman, M. L. (2005). Managing strategic contradictions: A top management model for managing innovation streams. *Organization Science, 16*(5), 522–36.

Stewart, A., & Hitt, M. A. (2012). Why can't a family business be more like a nonfamily business? Modes of professionalization in family firms. *Family Business Review, 25*(1), 58–86.

Stewart, A., & Miner, A. S. (2011). The prospects for family business in research universities. *Journal of Family Business Strategy, 2*(1), 3–14.

Stockmans, A., Lybaert, N., & Voordeckers, W. (2010). Socioemotional wealth and earnings management in private family firms. *Family Business Review, 23*(3), 280–94.

Strike, V. M., Berrone, P., Sapp, S. G., & Congiu, L. (2015). A socioemotional wealth approach to CEO career horizons in family firms. *Journal of Management Studies, 52*(4), 555–83.

Strike, V. M., & Rerup, C. (2016). Mediated sense making. *Academy of Management Journal, 59*(3), 880–905.

Stubner, S., Blarr, W. H., Brands, C., & Wulf, T. (2012). Organizational ambidexterity and family firm performance. *Journal of Small Business & Entrepreneurship, 25*(2), 217–29.

Suddaby, R., Coraiola, D., Harvey, C., & Foster, W. (2020). History and the micro-foundations of dynamic capabilities. *Strategic Management Journal*, *41*(3), 530–56.

Suddaby, R., & Foster, W. M. (2017). History and organizational change. *Journal of Management*, *43*(1), 19–38.

Suddaby, R., Foster, W. M., & Trank, C. Q. (2010). Rhetorical history as a source of competitive advantage. In J. A. C. Baum & J. Lampel (Eds.), *The globalization of strategy research* (pp. 147–73). Emerald Group.

Suddaby, R., & Jaskiewicz, P. (2020). Managing traditions: A critical capability for family business success. *Family Business Review*, *33*(3), 234–43.

Sundaramurthy, C., & Kreiner, G. E. (2008). Governing by managing identity boundaries: The case of family businesses. *Entrepreneurship Theory and Practice*, *32*(3), 415–36.

Swab, R. G., Sherlock, C., Markin, E., & Dibrell, C. (2020). "SEW" what do we know and where do we go? A review of socioemotional wealth and a way forward. *Family Business Review*, *33*(4), 424–45.

Tagiuri, R., & Davis, J. (1996). Bivalent attributes of the family firm. *Family Business Review*, *9*(2), 199–208.

Thornton, P. H. (2004). *Markets from culture: Institutional logics and organizational decisions in higher education publishing*. Stanford University Press.

Thornton, P. H., & Ocasio, W. (1999). Institutional logics and the historical contingency of power in organizations: Executive succession in the higher education publishing industry, 1958–1990. *American Journal of Sociology*, *105*(3), 801–43.

Tiscini, R., & Raoli, E. (2013). Stock option plan practices in family firms: The idiosyncratic private benefits approach. *Journal of Family Business Strategy*, *4*(2), 93–105.

Tolbert, P. S., David, R. J., & Sine, W. D. (2011). Studying choice and change: The intersection of institutional theory and entrepreneurship research. *Organization Science*, *22*(5), 1332–44.

Tracey, P., & Phillips, N. (2011). Entrepreneurship in emerging markets. *Management International Review*, *51*(1), 23–39.

Tsui, A. S. (2004). Contributing to global management knowledge: A case for high quality indigenous research. *Asia Pacific Journal of Management*, *21*(4), 491–513.

Upton, N., Vinton, K., Seaman, S., & Moore, C. (1993). Research note: Family business consultants—Who we are, what we do, and how we do it. *Family Business Review*, *6*(3), 301–11.

Vaara, E., Sonenshein, S., & Boje, D. (2016). Narratives as sources of stability and change in organizations: Approaches and directions for future research. *Academy of Management Annals, 10*(1), 495–560.

Vago, M. (2004). Integrated change management©: Challenges for family business clients and consultants. *Family Business Review, 17*(1), 71–80.

Vazquez, P., & Rocha, H. (2018). On the goals of family firms: A review and integration. *Journal of Family Business Strategy, 9*(2), 94–106.

Veider, V., & Matzler, K. (2016). The ability and willingness of family-controlled firms to arrive at organizational ambidexterity. *Journal of Family Business Strategy, 7*(2), 105–16.

Villalonga, B., & Amit, R. (2006). How do family ownership, control and management affect firm value? *Journal of Financial Economics, 80*(2), 385–417.

Ward, J. L. (1997). Growing the family business: Special challenges and best practices. *Family Business Review, 10*(4), 323–37.

Ward, J. L. (2004). *Perpetuating the family business: 50 lessons learned from long-lasting successful families in business.* Palgrave MacMillan.

Weber, M. (1947). *The theory of economic and social organization.* Oxford University Press.

Weigel, D. J., & Ballard-Reisch, D. S. (1997). Merging family and firm: An integrated systems approach to process and change. *Journal of Family and Economic Issues, 18*(1), 7–31.

Weik, E. (2019). Understanding institutional endurance: The role of dynamic form, harmony, and rhythm in institutions. *Academy of Management Review, 44*(2), 321–35.

Weismeier-Sammer, D. (2014). The role of familiness for family business innovativeness. *International Journal of Entrepreneurial Venturing, 6*(2), 101–17.

Welter, F., Baker, T., & Wirsching, K. (2019). Three waves and counting: the rising tide of contextualization in entrepreneurship research. *Small Business Economics, 52*(2), 319–30.

Westhead, P., & Cowling, M. (1998). Family firm research: The need for a methodological rethink. *Entrepreneurship Theory and Practice, 23*(1), 31–56.

Whetten, D., Foreman, P., & Dyer, W. G. (2014). Organizational identity and family business. In L. Melin, M. Nordqvist, & P. Sharma (Eds.). *The SAGE Handbook of Family Business* (pp. 480–97). Sage.

Whetten, D. A. (2006). Albert and Whetten revisited: Strengthening the concept of organizational identity. *Journal of Management Inquiry, 15*(3), 219–34.

Williamson, O. E. (1985). Assessing contract. *Journal of Law, Economics, & Organization, 1*(1), 177–208.

Winter, M., Fitzgerald, M. A., Heck, R. K., Haynes, G. W., & Danes, S. M. (1998). Revisiting the study of family businesses: Methodological challenges, dilemmas, and alternative approaches. *Family Business Review, 11*(3), 239–52.

Wiseman, R. M., & Gomez-Mejia, L. R. (1998). A behavioral agency model of managerial risk taking. *Academy of Management Review, 23*(1), 133–53.

Wry, T., Lounsbury, M., & Jennings, P. D. (2014). Hybrid vigor: Securing venture capital by spanning categories in nanotechnology. *Academy of Management Journal, 57*(5), 1309–33.

Xi, J. M., Kraus, S., Filser, M., & Kellermanns, F. W. (2015). Mapping the field of family business research: past trends and future directions. *International Entrepreneurship and Management Journal, 11*(1), 113–132.

Yu, A., Lumpkin, G. T., Sorenson, R. L., & Brigham, K. H. (2012). The landscape of family business outcomes: A summary and numerical taxonomy of dependent variables. *Family Business Review, 25*(1), 33–57.

Zahra, S. A. (2003). International expansion of US manufacturing family businesses: The effect of ownership and involvement. *Journal of Business Venturing, 18*(4), 495–512.

Zahra, S. A., Hayton, J. C., Neubaum, D. O., Dibrell, C., & Craig, J. (2008). Culture of family commitment and strategic flexibility: The moderating effect of stewardship. *Entrepreneurship Theory and Practice, 32*(6), 1035–54.

Zahra, S. A., & Sharma, P. (2004). Family business research: A strategic reflection. *Family Business Review, 17*(4), 331–346.

Zellweger, T. (2007). Time horizon, costs of equity capital, and generic investment strategies of firms. *Family Business Review, 20*(1), 1–15.

Zellweger, T. (2017). *Managing the family business: Theory and practice.* Edward Elgar.

Zellweger, T., Bird, M., & Weber, W. (2015). Global family business index. Available at www.alexandria.unisg.ch/240753/

Zellweger, T., Richards, M., Sieger, P., & Patel, P. C. (2016). How much am I expected to pay for my parents' firm? An institutional logics perspective on family discounts. *Entrepreneurship Theory and Practice, 40*(5), 1041–69.

Zellweger, T., Sieger, P., & Halter, F. (2011). Should I stay or should I go? Career choice intentions of students with family business background. *Journal of Business Venturing, 26*(5), 521–36.

Zellweger, T. M., Eddleston, K. A., & Kellermanns, F. W. (2010). Exploring the concept of familiness: Introducing family firm identity. *Journal of Family Business Strategy, 1*(1), 54–63.

Zellweger, T. M., Kellermanns, F. W., Eddleston, K. A., & Memili, E. (2012a). Building a family firm image: How family firms capitalize on their family ties. *Journal of Family Business Strategy, 3*(4), 239–50.

Zellweger, T. M., & Nason, R. S. (2008). A stakeholder perspective on family firm performance. *Family Business Review, 21*(3), 203–16.

Zellweger, T. M., Nason, R. S., & Nordqvist, M. (2012b). From longevity of firms to transgenerational entrepreneurship of families: Introducing family entrepreneurial orientation. *Family Business Review, 25*(2), 136–55.

Zellweger, T. M., Nason, R. S., Nordqvist, M., & Brush, C. G. (2013). Why do family firms strive for nonfinancial goals? An organizational identity perspective. *Entrepreneurship Theory and Practice, 37*(2), 229–48.

Zhao, E. Y. (2022). *Optimal distinctiveness: A new agenda for the study of competitive positioning of organizations and markets.* Cambridge University Press.

Zhao, E. Y., Fisher, G., Lounsbury, M., & Miller, D. (2017). Optimal distinctiveness: Broadening the interface between institutional theory and strategic management. *Strategic Management Journal, 38*(1), 93–113.

Zody, Z., Sprenkle, D., MacDermid, S., & Schrank, H. (2006). Boundaries and the functioning of family and business systems. *Journal of Family and Economic Issues, 27*(2), 185–206.

Zuckerman, E. W. (1999). The categorical imperative: Securities analysts and the illegitimacy discount. *American Journal of Sociology, 104*(5), 1398–438.

Zuckerman, E. W. (2016). Optimal distinctiveness revisited. In M. G. Pratt, M. Schultz, B. E. Ashforth, & D. Ravasi (Eds.), *The Oxford handbook of organizational identity* (pp. 183–99). Oxford University Press.

Cambridge Elements $\equiv$

Organization Theory

Nelson Phillips
UC Santa Barbara

Nelson Phillips is Professor of Technology Management at UC Santa Barbara. His research interests include organization theory, technology strategy, innovation, and entrepreneurship, often studied from an institutional theory perspective.

Royston Greenwood
Imperial College London, University of Alberta

Royston Greenwood is the Telus Professor of Strategic Management at the University of Alberta, a visiting professor at the University of Cambridge, and a visiting professor at the University of Edinburgh. His research interests include organizational change and professional misconduct.

About the Series

Organization theory covers many different approaches to understanding organizations. Its focus is on what constitutes the how and why of organizations and organizing, bringing understanding of organizations in a holistic way. The purpose of Elements in Organization Theory is to systematize and contribute to our understanding of organizations.

Cambridge Elements ☰

Organization Theory

Elements in the Series

Printed in the United States
by Baker & Taylor Publisher Services